BIG IDEAS
OF SCIENCE
REFERENCE LIBRARY

PEARSON

Boston, Massachusetts
Chandler, Arizona
Glenview, Illinois
Upper Saddle River, New Jersey

CONTENTS

Big Ideas of
   Earth Science vi

Big Ideas of
   Life Science viii

Big Ideas of
   Physical Science x

Plant Tricks xii

Plastic 2

Pluto 4

Population Growth 6

Predicting Hurricanes 8

Pregnancy 10

Probability 12

Prosthetic Limb 14

Puberty 16

Quarks and Leptons 18

Quasars 20

Racehorses 22

Radio 24

Rainbows 26

Rain Forest 28

Rats 32

Recycling 34

Red Tide 36

Redwoods 38

Renewal 40

Rheumatoid Arthritis ... 42

Robots 44

Roller Coaster 46

Rube Goldberg
   Devices 48

Rubies 50

Sailing 52

Satellite Dish 54

Saturn 56

Scent Pollution 58

Science at Work 60

Scorpion 62

Sea Horse 64

Sea Stacks 66

Sea Turtles 68

Seals 70

Seaweed 72

Seed Bank 74

Sharks 76

Shelter 78

Simulators 80

Singing 82

Skeletons 84

Skin 86

Skydiving 88

Skyscrapers 90

Skywalk 92

Sleep 94

Sloth 96

Snakes 98

Credits 100

KEY
These symbols appear in the top right corner below the topic name
to connect the topic to the branches of science.

 Earth Science   Life Science   Physical Science

BIG IDEAS OF EARTH SCIENCE 🌍

The Big Ideas of earth science help us understand our changing planet, its long history, and its place in the universe. Earth scientists study Earth and the forces that change its surface and interior.

Earth is part of a system of objects that orbit the sun.

Asteroids
Astronomy Myths
Bay of Fundy
Comets
Constellations
Earth
Gravity
Jupiter's Moons
Mars
Mars Rover
Mercury
Meteorites
Moon
Neptune
Pluto
Saturn
Solar Eclipse
Solar Power
Space Probes
Summer Solstice
Uranus
Venus

Earth is 4.6 billion years old and the rock record contains its history.

Atmosphere
Dating Rocks
Deep Sea Vents
Dinosaurs
Eryops
Extinction
Family Tree
Fossils
Geologic Time
Giant Mammals
Ice Age

Earth's land, water, air, and life form a system.

Altitude
Atacama Desert
Atmosphere
Aurora Borealis
Buoys
Doppler Radar
Dust Storms
Earth's Core
Floods
Fog
Gliding
Predicting Hurricanes
Rainbows
Sailing
Snowmaking
Storm Chasing
Thunderstorms
Weather Fronts

Earth is the water planet.

Amazon River
Beaches
Drinking Water
Everglades
Great Lakes
Mid-Ocean Ridge
Niagara Falls
Ocean Currents
Sea Stacks
Surfing
Thermal Imaging
Tsunami
Upwelling
Water

Earth is a continually changing planet.

Acid Rain
Afar Triangle
Caves
Coal

Colorado Plateau
Colorado River
Coral Reefs
Crystals
Dunes
Earthquakes
Equator
Fluorescent Minerals
Geocaching
Geodes
Geysers
Glaciers
Gold Mining
Hoodoos
Ice Age
Islands
Kilauea
Landslides
Lava
Mapping
Marble Quarries
Mid-Ocean Ridge
Mount Everest
Niagara Falls
Rain Forest
Rubies
Sea Stacks
Soil
Terrace Farming
Tour de France
Tsunami

Human activities can change Earth's land, water, air, and life.

Air Pollution
Energy Conservation
Equator
Fuel Cell Cars
Global Warming
Ice Age
Ocean Currents
Rain Forest
Shelter

The universe is very old, very large, and constantly changing.

Big Bang Theory
Black Holes
Constellations
Hubble Space Telescope
Milky Way
Quasars
Universe

Science, technology, and society affect each other.

Astronauts
Hubble Space Telescope
Jetpacks
International Space
  Station
Mars Rover
Predicting Hurricanes
Robots
Satellite Dish
Science at Work
Space Technology
Space Tourism
Virtual World

Scientists use mathematics in many ways.

Buoys
Doppler Radar
Mars Rover
Measurement
Neptune

Scientists use scientific inquiry to explain the natural world.

Extinction
Predicting Hurricanes
Wind Power
Neptune

BIG IDEAS OF LIFE SCIENCE

Life scientists study organisms, their life processes, and how they interact with one another and their environment. The Big Ideas of life science help us understand how living things are organized, how they get and use energy, and how they reproduce.

Living things grow, change, and reproduce during their lifetimes.

Animal Communication
Bush Baby
Courtship Rituals
Echolocation
Gorillas
Hummingbirds
Hypothalamus
Instinct
Marsupials
Menstrual Cycle
Penguins
Pregnancy
Puberty
Sea Horse
Seals
Sleep
Sloth
Tasmanian Devil
Twins
Worms

Living things are made of cells.

Blood Types
Cactus
Cell Division
Microscopes
Quarks and Leptons
Scent Pollution
Skeletons

Living things are alike yet different.

Adaptations
Aerogels
Bacteria
Bats
Bears
Cactus
Common Cold
DNA Connections
Exoskeleton
Family Tree
Farming
Ferns
Flowers
Frankenfoods
Fungi
Geckos
Giant Mammals
Gila Monster
Insects
Jellyfish
Naming
Patterns in Nature
Plant Tricks
Rain Forest
Red Tide
Redwoods
Scent Pollution
Skeletons
Snakes
Soil
Spiders
Survival
Symmetry
Taco Science
Whales

Living things interact with their environment.

Acid Rain
Air Pollution
Amazon River
Atacama Desert
Bats
Bay of Fundy
Beaches
Biodiversity
Biofuels
Bush Baby
Butterflies
Camouflage
Coal
Colorado Plateau
Deep Sea Vents
Energy Conservation
Everglades
Farming
Forestry
Frozen Zoo
Fuel Cell Cars
Georges Bank

Global Warming
GPS Tracking
Great Lakes
Hybrid Vehicles
Insects
Islands
Kilauea
Light Bulbs
Mid-Ocean Ridge
Mount Everest
Oil Spills
Patterns in Nature
Plant Invasion
Plastic
Population Growth
Rain Forest
Recycling
Red Tide
Renewal
Sea Horse
Seaweed
Seed Bank
Sharks
Shelter
Skywalk

Sloth
Soil
Solar Power
Supercooling Frogs
Sushi
Upwelling
Vultures

Genetic information passes from parents to offspring.

Blood Types
Colorblindness
DNA Evidence
Frankenfoods
Frozen Zoo
Genetic Disorders
Human Genome Project
Hummingbirds
Mutations
Probability

Living things get and use energy.

Algae
Barracuda
Birds
Cell Division
Elephants
Hummingbirds
New Body Parts
Octopus
Scorpion
Sea Horse
Seals
Sour Milk
Tasmanian Devil
Teeth

Structures in living things are related to their functions.

ACL Tear
Aerobic Exercise
ALS
Altitude
Animal Bodies
Birds
Blood Pressure
Blood Types
Brain Power
Broken Bones
Defibrillators
Digestion
Dolphins
Drinking Water
Exoskeleton
Fats

Gliding
Hearing Loss
Heartbeat
Hummingbirds
Jellyfish
Kidney Transplant
Laser Eye Surgery
Left vs. Right Brain
Marsupials
No Smoking
Open-Heart Surgery
Prosthetic Limb
Scent Pollution
Sea Turtles
Simulators
Singing
Skeletons
Skin
Sleep
Sloth
Steroids
Superfoods
Teeth
The Bends
Tour de France
Tweeters and Woofers
Vitamins and Minerals
Weightlifting

Living things change over time.

DNA Connections
Family Tree
Gorillas
Islands
Madagascar
Racehorses

Living things maintain constant conditions inside their bodies.

Allergies
Astronauts
Cancer Treatment
Common Cold
HIV/AIDS
Malaria
Marathon Training
Mold
MRI
Pandemic
Rats
Rheumatoid Arthritis
Scent Pollution
Sleep
Thermal Imaging
Vaccines
Working Body

Scientists use mathematics in many ways.

Census
Estimation
Hazardous Materials
Measurement
Probability
Simulators

Science, technology, and society affect each other.

Biomimetics
Clinical Trials
DNA Evidence
Eye Scan
Human Genome Project
Prosthetic Limb
Robots
Science at Work
Truth in Advertising

Scientists use scientific inquiry to explain the natural world.

BPA
Crittercam
Forensics
Human Genome Project
Naming
Quarks and Leptons
Truth in Advertising

BIG IDEAS OF PHYSICAL SCIENCE

Physical scientists study matter and energy. The Big Ideas of physical science help us describe the objects we see around us and understand their properties, motions, and interactions.

A net force causes an object's motion to change.

Asteroids
Astronauts
Bridges
Collision
Crew
Drag Racing
Formula 1 Car
Gravitron
Gravity
Hockey
Hovercraft
Jetpacks
Meteorites
Quasars
Roller Coaster
Sailing
Skydiving
Snowboard
Tour de France

Energy can take different forms but is always conserved.

Aerogels
ALS
Aurora Borealis
Bicycles
Black Holes
Bridges
Bungee Jumping
Catapults
Cordless Drill
Crew
Defibrillators
Earth's Core
Energy Conservation
Geocaching
Gliding
Headphones
Hoover Dam
Hybrid Vehicles
Lichtenberg Figures
Lifting Electromagnets
Light Bulbs
Microscopes
MP3 Player
MRI
Niagara Falls
Radio
Roller Coaster
Rube Goldberg Devices
Skyscraper
Skywalk
Submarines
Taco Science
Thermal Imaging
Weightlifting

Waves transmit energy.

Animal Communication
Cellphone
Color
Digital Camera
Doppler Radar
Echolocation
Eye Scan
Fluorescent Minerals
Geocaching
GPS Tracking
Guitar
Headphones
Hearing Loss
Holograms
Hubble Space Telescope
Hummingbirds
Laser Eye Surgery
Lighthouse
Microscopes
Mirages
Night Vision Goggles
Predicting Hurricanes
Radio
Rainbows
Rubies
Satellite Dish
Sea Stacks
Seaweed
Singing
Solar Power
Sonic Booms
Surfing
Thunderstorms
Tsunami
Tweeters and Woofers
Virtual World

Atoms are the building blocks of matter.

Acid Rain
Black Holes
Body Protection
Caves
Creating Elements
Crystals
Geckos
Glass

Gold Mining
Mars Rover
Melting Point
Meteorites
Nuclear Medicine
Prosthetic Limb
Quarks and Leptons
Steel
The Bends
Water

Mass and energy are conserved during physical and chemical changes.

Digestion
Earth
Fire Extinguishers
Fireworks
Forestry
Hovercraft
Ice Houses
   Lava
     Melting Point
     Scent Pollution
     Snowmaking
     Supercooling
       Frogs
      The Bends

Scientists use mathematics in many ways.

Buoys
Hazardous Materials
Mars Rover
Measurement
Wind Tunnel

Scientists use scientific inquiry to explain the natural world.

Biomimetics
Forensics
Quarks and Leptons
Wind Power

Science, technology, and society affect each other.

Bridges
Cellphone
Formula 1 Car
Hubble Space
   Telescope
Light Bulbs
Prosthetic Limb
Robots
Science at Work

PLANT TRICKS

You might think all plants rely only on photosynthesis or absorb all their nutrients from the soil. Think again! Plants live in a wide variety of biomes and habitats such as forest, desert, and marsh. They have evolved adaptations, characteristics that help them survive in stressful environments. Some plant adaptations are especially unique. Places like rain forests and many swamps, for example, have very little fertile soil. Plants that inhabit these places cannot depend on the soil to fulfill all their nutritional needs. They must find other ways to survive. Some live on nutrients left in the dead matter of other plants. Others actually trap, kill, and digest insects. Because some plants like Indian pipe (white waxy plants) lack chlorophyll, they cannot make their own food to live. Instead, they have a parasitic relationship with fungi, where the plant's roots tap into the fungi and take the nutrients they need.

VENUS' FLYTRAP ▼

The Venus' flytrap lives in certain boggy areas of North and South Carolina. Because the soil cannot provide all its nutrients, the Venus' flytrap evolved as a carnivorous plant. Carnivorous plants are adapted to attract, capture, digest, and absorb insects and other tiny animals. The flytrap's jawlike leaves secrete sweet-smelling nectar. When an unsuspecting insect tickles the trigger hairs, the leaves snap shut. Digestive fluids break down the insect's soft parts, and the leaves absorb the nutrients. The plant releases the exoskeleton days later.

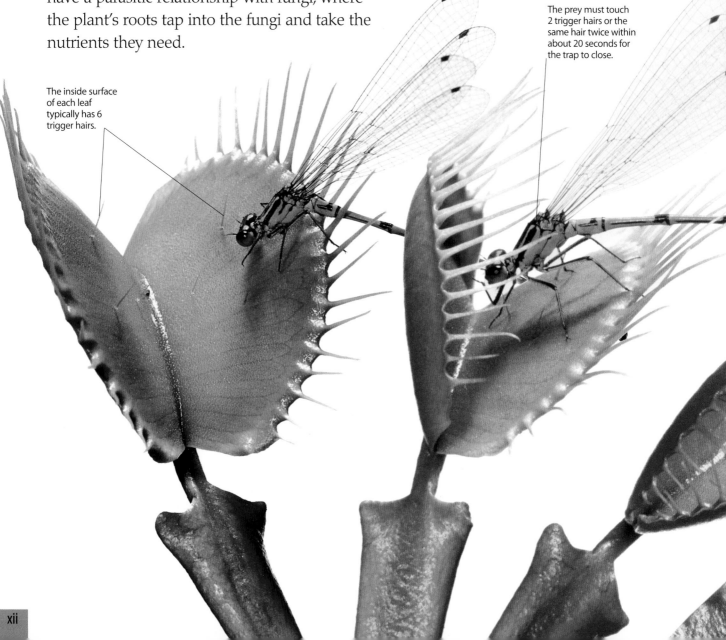

The inside surface of each leaf typically has 6 trigger hairs.

The prey must touch 2 trigger hairs or the same hair twice within about 20 seconds for the trap to close.

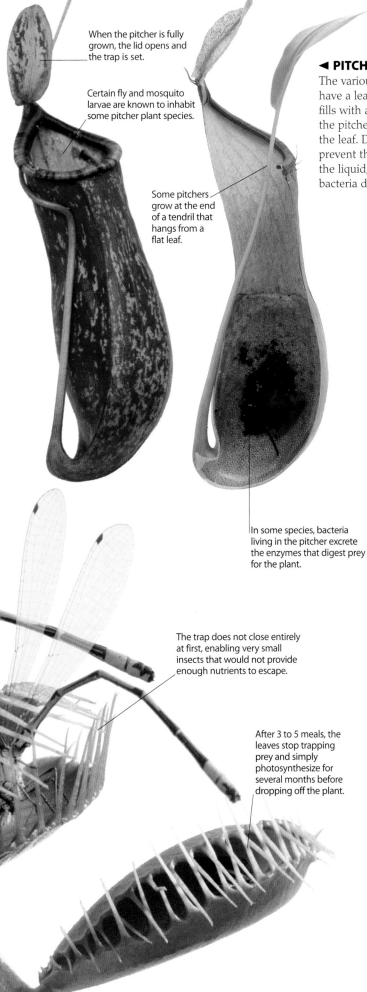

When the pitcher is fully grown, the lid opens and the trap is set.

Certain fly and mosquito larvae are known to inhabit some pitcher plant species.

Some pitchers grow at the end of a tendril that hangs from a flat leaf.

In some species, bacteria living in the pitcher excrete the enzymes that digest prey for the plant.

The trap does not close entirely at first, enabling very small insects that would not provide enough nutrients to escape.

After 3 to 5 meals, the leaves stop trapping prey and simply photosynthesize for several months before dropping off the plant.

◄ PITCHER PLANT

The various species of carnivorous pitcher plants evolved to have a leaf shaped like a tall pitcher or cup. The leaf partially fills with a fragrant liquid that attracts prey. Once inside the pitcher, the prey slides down the slippery lower walls of the leaf. Downward pointing hairs above the slippery sides prevent the prey from escaping. After the prey drowns in the liquid, acid from digested prey or enzymes produced by bacteria digest the prey and the leaf absorbs the nutrients.

did you know?..

BROMELIADS ARE LIKE SMALL ECOSYSTEMS. BIRDS, TREE FROGS, TINY CRABS, AND OTHER CREATURES MIGHT SPEND THEIR ENTIRE LIVES INSIDE THEM.

AIR PLANTS ▲

Bromeliads, also called *air plants,* do not need soil. Instead they use their roots to cling to a host plant. Bromeliads get all the moisture and nutrients they need from the air and from leaves and debris that fall into them. Their leaves form a tight spiral, capturing water from dew or a rainstorm. They also are home to insects that excrete wastes full of nutrients.

PLASTIC

Bottles, toothbrushes, computers, backpacks, food packaging, media players, and CDs: what do each of these items contain? Plastic! It's strong, lightweight, inexpensive, durable, and has countless uses. In 2002, about 107 billion pounds of plastic were produced in North America alone. There are many kinds of plastic, but each belongs to one of two main categories: thermoplastics or thermosets. Thermoplastics, such as bottles for drinks, melt when they are heated and harden when they cool. Thermosets, such as two-part epoxy glue, are hardened by heat or chemical interaction. They retain their shape even when reheated. Most plastics are made from chemicals produced during the oil refining process. If these plastics are thrown away, they remain in the environment for a long time. But recycling plastics allows them to be turned into many useful products.

◄ R IS FOR RECYCLING

More than one third of all plastic is used for disposable goods, such as bottles and bags. Much of this ends up in landfills or as litter, but some of it could be recycled. Because thermoplastics can be heated and reformed repeatedly, they can be recycled into other products. The type of product depends upon the type of plastic. For example, polyethylene terephthalate (PET) water bottles can be turned into fleece jackets and blankets, high-density polyethylene (HDPE) milk bottles can become floor tiles, and polystyrene (PS) compact disc jackets can become egg cartons. PET is light and airtight, good for carbonated beverages. HDPE is tougher and resistant to solvents. PS is rigid and can be "foamed" to form insulation.

◄ FROM MILK BOTTLES TO LAWN CHAIRS

It looks like wood, but the lumber used to build these chairs is actually made of recycled high-density polyethylene that has been ground into flakes, dyed, melted, and remolded into boards. Other types of recycled plastic lumber are made from blending different types of plastic, adding fiberglass, adding wood, or adding materials such as flax or rice hulls. Plastic lumber is used to make a variety of products, including tables, fencing, signs, decks, house siding, boardwalks, and railroad ties. Plastic lumber has even been used to build bridges for cars!

MOLDED INTO SHAPE ▲

Plastic products can be made using a number of different methods. For example, some cups are made using a process known as vacuum forming. First, a sheet of plastic is attached to a frame, warmed, and then sucked into a mold. As the plastic cools, it hardens into the shape of the mold. After it cools, it is separated from the mold, trimmed, and finished. This process is used to make many other items such as the inside of refrigerators and bathtubs, as well as packaging for chocolates and cosmetics.

Both the frames and lenses of these retro sunglasses are made of plastic.

did you
know?..................
SEA TURTLES THINK FLOATING PLASTIC BAGS ARE JELLYFISH. THOUSANDS OF SEA TURTLES DIE EVERY YEAR FROM EATING THEM.

Bottles like these can be made by forcing air into a bubble of hot, soft plastic inside a mold.

◄ EVERYWHERE AROUND US

Plastics can be rigid, flexible, rubbery, soft, tough, or even slippery! They appear in many places that we might not expect: bicycle tires, fishing line, glues, wind turbines, armored vehicles, and spacecraft. There are a great many types of plastic, each with different properties and applications. Fiberglass, nylon, PVC, styrofoam, nonstick coating, Gore-Tex®, and Kevlar®—these are all plastics. Most are cheap, lightweight, hygienic, and easy to produce. No wonder they appear almost everywhere we look!

From the time of its discovery in 1930, Pluto was the ninth planet in our solar system. But science changes, and some things are hard to let go. That's what happened in 2006 when astronomers decided to stop classifying Pluto as a planet. Why? A celestial body must meet three characteristics to be called a planet: it must orbit the sun, it must be round, and it must have cleared away any other objects in its orbit. Pluto comes close, but it has other objects occupying its orbit. Therefore, scientists now call Pluto a dwarf planet. Pluto also has three small moons named Charon, Hydra, and Nix. The space probe New Horizons, sent by NASA in 2006 to explore Pluto and its moons, will arrive in 2015. It's a long trip because the dwarf planet is about 3.6 billion miles (about 5.8 billion km) away from the sun. That's about 39 times farther than Earth is from the sun!

The distant sun would look much dimmer from Pluto than it would from Earth.

did you know? PLUTO IS SO SMALL ITS DIAMETER IS ONLY ABOUT HALF THE WIDTH OF THE UNITED STATES.

Scientists think that Charon's surface is covered in frozen water, while Pluto's surface is probably a frozen mixture of methane, nitrogen, and carbon monoxide.

PLUTO FROM CHARON

The background scene shows how the sun and Pluto would look if you were standing on the surface of Charon (below). Just as our moon shows only one side to Earth, Charon shows only one side to Pluto. Pluto also rotates so that it shows only one side to Charon at all times! This is called *tidal locking*. It happens because Charon's orbit around Pluto takes about 6.5 Earth days, and one full rotation of Pluto also takes about 6.5 Earth days.

Solar System

Mercury   Earth

Venus   Mars

Sun

Jupiter

Saturn

Uranus   Neptune

Pluto

The dwarf planet Pluto is compared with the 8 planets of our solar system.

When Pluto is farthest from the sun, its atmosphere freezes and falls to the ground.

HOW BIG IS PLUTO? ▶

When you look at a planet, you probably think of something that is much larger than Earth's moon. Pluto's diameter is about 1,441 miles (2,320 km), making it smaller than Earth's moon. Charon, Pluto's largest moon, has a diameter of about 790 miles (about 1, 270 km), about half the size of Pluto. Farther away than Pluto, astronomers have discovered two small objects that orbit our sun at the very fringe of the solar system. They have named them *Sedna*, after the Inuit goddess of sea creatures, and *Quaoar*, the god of creation of the Tongva people of California.

Sedna
(800–1,100 miles
in diameter)

Quaoar
(800 miles)

Pluto
(1,400 miles)

Moon
(2,100 miles)

Earth
(8,000 miles)

POPULATION GROWTH

More than 6.7 billion people make up the world's population. Will we have enough resources such as food, energy, and land to support an estimated population of 9 billion people by 2050? Scientists called *demographers* study changes in population size over time, and factors that affect the rate of population change. Populations continue to grow as long as the number of births each year is greater than the number of deaths. In an idealized world with unlimited resources, a population grows at an increasing rate. But populations cannot grow indefinitely; they will eventually deplete natural resources. In the natural world, population growth slows when a population reaches carrying capacity, the maximum population size that the environment is able to sustain indefinitely. Carrying capacity has regulating factors including availability of food, water, and space. Highly populated nations face challenging decisions in response to questions like these: Will we reach carrying capacity? Will our resources run out?

BEYOND CARRYING CAPACITY ▼
India's population is greater than 1.1 billion, making it the second most populated country in the world. High population growth has put a tremendous strain on the country's resources. The percentage of the population that lives below the poverty line has decreased in the past 30 years from about 50 to 25 percent. However, the population has doubled in that time, so the number of people living in poverty has not decreased.

did you know?
MORE THAN 370,000 INDIVIDUALS ARE BORN EACH DAY.

India 2000	India 2025	India 2050

Male · Age group · Female (repeated for each graph)

Age groups: 100+, 95-99, 90-94, 85-89, 80-84, 75-79, 70-74, 65-69, 60-64, 55-59, 50-54, 45-49, 40-44, 35-39, 30-34, 25-29, 20-24, 15-19, 10-14, 5-9, 0-4

Population (in millions): 70 60 50 40 30 20 10 0 0 10 20 30 40 50 60 70

▲ CHANGING THE SHAPE OF POPULATION GROWTH

The age structure graphs above show the number of males and females in each age group in India. The first graph shows actual populations in the year 2000, while the second two graphs show predictions. India's age structure indicates rapid growth of younger populations. This is common in developing countries where birth rates are high and living conditions are harsh. Predictions show birth rates stabilizing while the older population increases dramatically.

LIMITING THE NUMBER OF CHILDREN ▼

China has the largest human population in the world, with more than 1.3 billion people. Its population could have been greater, but in 1979, concerns arose about the effects of rapid population growth on economic and social resources. In response, the Chinese government introduced a one child per family policy. The policy has significantly reduced birth rates.

PREDICTING HURRICANES

Hurricanes are one of nature's most destructive storms. Long ago, people had no way of knowing when a hurricane was approaching. In 1900, a hurricane struck Galveston, Texas, and 6,000 or more people died when the island was flooded. Such a loss is unlikely today, because forecasters can predict 5 days in advance how strong hurricanes will be and where they might make landfall. How do forecasters know so much about hurricanes? They use modern equipment like satellites, airplanes, radar, ocean buoys, and sophisticated computer modeling systems. Satellites can see the ocean where there are few ships. They can track cloud formations and ocean temperatures. Doppler radar can monitor wind data and precipitation levels. Ocean buoys send back data on air and water temperature, wave height, and wind speed. Airplanes drop tiny weather stations into the storm to get up-to-date information. Complicated computer programs analyze all the data to predict hurricane behavior.

did you know?
....
THE MOST DESTRUCTIVE PORTION OF A HURRICANE IS FOUND IN THE EYE WALL—WHICH BORDERS THE CALMEST PART OF THE HURRICANE, THE EYE.

LOOKING INTO HURRICANE IVAN
NASA's Tropical Rainfall Measuring Mission (TRMM) satellite, originally designed to measure rainfall, allows scientists to see rain patterns inside hurricanes. With TRMM, meteorologists can better forecast hurricane intensity. Hurricane Ivan (shown in the large background image) was one of the worst Atlantic hurricanes ever recorded. Ivan caused enormous damage and spawned 117 tornadoes in the United States. Because storm forecasts were so accurate, however, fewer than 100 people died.

❶ HURRICANE RITA ENTERS THE GULF OF MEXICO Ocean regions that have sea surface temperatures of 82°F (almost 28°C) or more (indicated as red and orange areas) are warm enough to form a hurricane.

❷ RITA GATHERS STRENGTH The hurricane winds are strengthened by the heat energy from the warm ocean. Sea surface temperatures cool as the hurricane passes.

❸ RITA MAKES LANDFALL Rita makes landfall on the Texas-Louisiana border. Because the ocean no longer supplies energy, Rita quickly downgrades from an intense hurricane to a tropical storm.

The National Oceanic and Atmospheric Administration (NOAA) monitors the Western Hemisphere with satellites similar to this one.

STORM CHASERS ▲

Some experienced meteorologists pursue severe weather events in trucks called *Dopplers on Wheels* (DOW). They use radar to collect data from inside storm cells. This up-to-the-minute, localized storm information is added to other collected data to help scientists forecast the weather more accurately. DOWs have shed light on how hurricanes intensify. Here, a DOW collects data as Hurricane Frances approaches Florida in 2004.

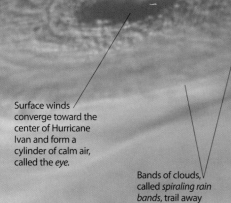

Surface winds converge toward the center of Hurricane Ivan and form a cylinder of calm air, called the *eye.*

Bands of clouds, called *spiraling rain bands,* trail away from a ring of tall thunderstorms surrounding the eye.

SATELLITE WEATHER OBSERVATION ▲

The United States uses stationary and polar-orbiting satellites to observe weather and other phenomena 24 hours a day. These satellites track fast-breaking storms and tornadoes in the country's interior and tropical storms in the Atlantic and Pacific oceans. This 3-D model made from a satellite image of Hurricane Wilma shows its eye and rings of moderate to intense rain. Red portions indicate areas of heaviest rainfall. At the time of this image, Wilma had sustained wind speeds of 150 miles per hour (about 241 km/h).

PREGNANCY

Human babies begin life inside the mother. This period of gestation is called *pregnancy*. It lasts about 40 weeks, or 9 months. For the first 8 weeks of pregnancy, the developing baby is called an *embryo*. After 8 weeks, it is called a *fetus*. The developing baby grows within an amniotic sac in the mother's uterus. This sac is filled with fluid that protects and cushions the baby. An umbilical cord connects the baby to the placenta, a thick cushion of tissue that provides a constant supply of nutrients and oxygen from the mother. The placenta allows a developing baby to stay within the safety of the mother's body for 9 months. This gives the heart, lungs, and other organs time to develop fully so they can function on their own at the time of birth.

A HUMAN FETUS AT 31 WEEKS ▶

At 4 weeks, the brain, spinal cord, and heart have begun to form. By 8 weeks, the heart is beating steadily, and at 12 weeks, the fetus can make a fist. By 20 weeks, the fetus can hear, swallow, and even scratch itself with tiny fingernails. By 31 weeks, it kicks and jabs. Its bones are soft, but fully formed, and it weighs around 3.5 pounds (1.6 kg).

did you know? ....
THE HEAVIEST NEWBORN RECORDED WEIGHED MORE THAN 22 POUNDS (10 KG). THE LIGHTEST TO SURVIVE WEIGHED 8.6 OUNCES (244 G).

LABOR AND DELIVERY ▶

When a baby is ready to be born, the muscles in the mother's uterus begin to contract at intervals, a process called *labor*. Because the baby is being squeezed, its heart rate has to be monitored to make sure it is getting enough oxygen during the delivery. A fetal monitor records the baby's heart rate.

Printed record of the baby's heartbeat

◀ CAN A FETUS HEAR MUSIC?

Sounds pass through the amniotic fluid and stimulate the fetus's hearing by being conducted through the bones of the skull. Studies show that the fetus can detect low-frequency sounds, but no one knows if the fetus can hear music. PET scans and other images of brain activity may help scientists answer this question.

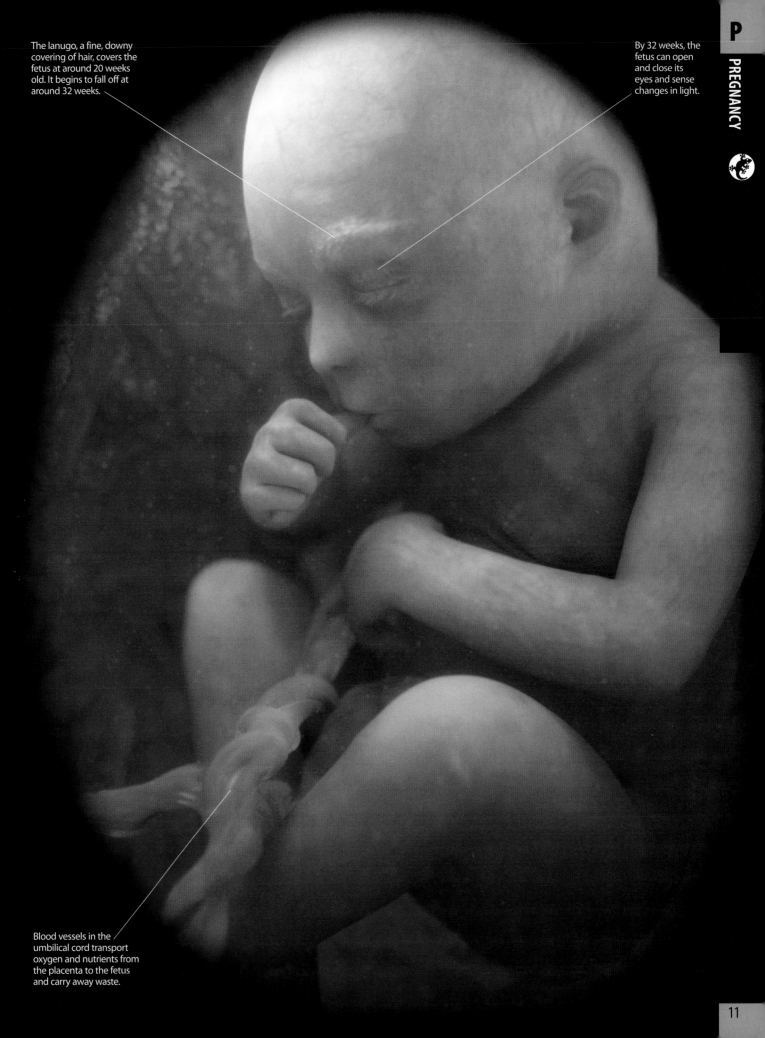

The lanugo, a fine, downy covering of hair, covers the fetus at around 20 weeks old. It begins to fall off at around 32 weeks.

By 32 weeks, the fetus can open and close its eyes and sense changes in light.

Blood vessels in the umbilical cord transport oxygen and nutrients from the placenta to the fetus and carry away waste.

PROBABILITY

Think of a number between 1 and 6. If you roll a die, what's the probability that you'll roll the number you thought of? It's 1 in 6 or the fraction $\frac{1}{6}$! Probability is the branch of mathematics that helps us understand events that depend on chance. While the study of probability began with an interest in games, people use probability today to assess the chance of a baby having a genetic disease or to predict the likelihood of a storm.

Glass eyes

Identical twins are produced when a fertilized egg divides in two, a probability of 1 in 250 births. They are not perfectly identical even though their genes are usually identical. Eye color can sometimes be different because of changes that occur during development.

◄ WHAT COLOR?

There are at least three genes that determine eye color. Each of these genes has two alleles, which are different forms of the gene. For example, one of the eye-color genes, the brown-blue gene, has one allele that may result in brown eyes and another allele that may result in blue eyes. Children inherit one allele from each parent for every gene. A Punnett square, which shows the allele pairs that can result from crossing two parent's genes, can be used to find a particular outcome's probability. For example, using *B* for brown and *b* for blue, suppose both parents have alleles *Bb*. There are 4 equally likely outcomes (2 are the same): *BB, Bb, Bb,* and *bb*. The probability that the offspring will have alleles *BB* is ¼. The allele for brown eyes, *B*, is dominant over blue, so if even one *B* allele is present, the children will have brown eyes. So, in our example, the children will have a 3 out of 4 probability of having brown eyes. Of course, it's not that simple, because there are other genes involved that determine green eyes, hazel eyes, all of the other eye colors. However, this is how geneticists determine the probability of inheriting different traits.

did you know?
ONE STUDY SUGGESTS THAT PEOPLE ORIGINALLY HAD ONLY BROWN EYES. BLUE EYES ARE THE RESULT OF A GENETIC MUTATION IN AN INDIVIDUAL SOME 6,000 TO 10,000 YEARS AGO.

PROSTHETIC LIMB

People have used prosthetic limbs to replace body parts since ancient times. Today's prostheses have come a long way from the carved wood and leather toe found on one Egyptian mummy! Many are fairly basic structures made of plastic and metal. Others include electronic sensors. Some foot and leg prosthetics can sense the way a wearer walks. It then adjusts the movement of the prosthesis so walking is easier and more comfortable. The wearer can customize a prosthetic leg by choosing an artificial foot ideal for the activities he or she does. An international team, led by the U.S. government, has been developing artificial arms. These prostheses can move like natural arms, grasp delicate objects, and even feel. Instead of using the muscles in their chests or shoulders to operate the arm, wearers can run these prostheses with a thought—the same way they controlled their natural limb.

know? did you
SOMETIMES AMPUTEES EXPERIENCE "PHANTOM LIMB" SENSATIONS, A FEELING THAT THEIR LIMB IS STILL THERE EVEN THOUGH IT HAS BEEN AMPUTATED.

▼ BIONIC HAND

For years, prosthetic hands were simply hooks, or artificial hands on which only two fingers and the thumb moved. Not any more. Lindsay Block wears a new prosthesis called the i-LIMB™ Hand. When covered with a custom skinlike material, the i-LIMB Hand looks natural. Lindsay controls the fingers by contracting and relaxing the muscles in her arm. Now she can do everything from picking up a coffee cup to putting her bank card in an ATM.

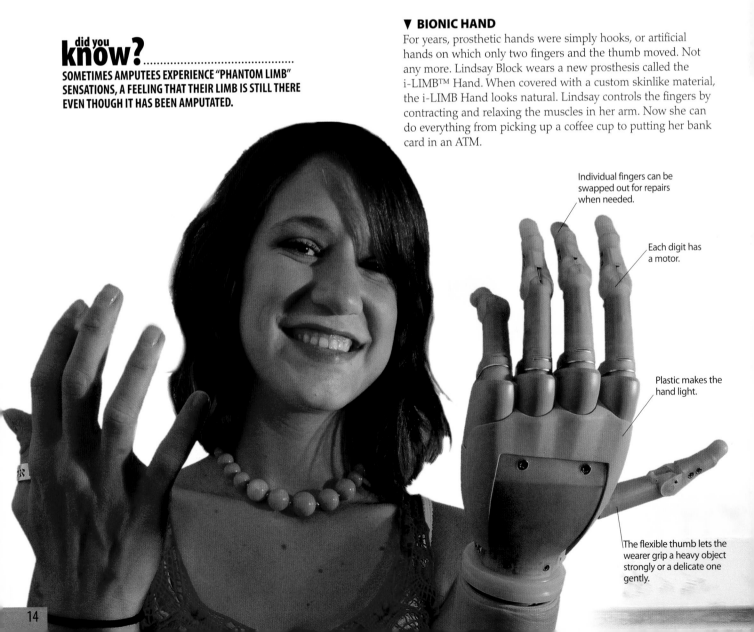

Individual fingers can be swapped out for repairs when needed.

Each digit has a motor.

Plastic makes the hand light.

The flexible thumb lets the wearer grip a heavy object strongly or a delicate one gently.

Prostheses attach to the stump of the limb.

Newer prosthetic ankles can flex naturally.

Prosthetic feet can be switched out.

▲ RUNNING LIKE A CHEETAH

South African athlete Oscar Pistorius has been called "the fastest thing on no legs." He wears a prosthetic called the Össur Flex-Foot Cheetah®. It was invented by Van Phillips, who studied the way animals' limbs compress and stretch. The feet, made of high-tech carbon fiber, are strong, flexible, and light. His success has caused controversy because some people claim the prostheses give him an advantage over other competitors.

◄ GOING FOR GOLD

In 2001, Casey Tibbs lost his right leg below the knee in a motorcycle accident. Now he competes in international competitions in track and field, winning gold and silver medals. Casey wears different prostheses depending on whether he's running or throwing the shot put or discus. He works for the U.S. Navy, helping personnel who have been injured or who lost limbs recover from their injuries.

PUBERTY

Are you moody? Do you sleep a lot? Are there pimples on your skin each morning? You may be going through puberty, the time when each person becomes sexually mature. Puberty begins during adolescence, the time between childhood and adulthood. In boys, it usually starts between the ages of 12 and 16. It begins earlier for girls, usually between the ages of 10 and 14. Puberty begins when a part of the brain called the *hypothalamus* releases a hormone that signals a pea-sized gland called the *pituitary* to release other hormones. These hormones trigger physical and emotional changes that include a growth spurt; the growth of pubic hair; the growth of breasts and the onset of menstruation in girls; and muscle development, the appearance of facial hair, and a deepening voice in boys. Puberty can be stressful, but your body will make it through these changes. You will emerge in good shape!

SKIN FLARE-UPS ▶

Hormones released during puberty cause oil glands under the skin to become more active. This increased oil production can clog pores, creating pimples or acne. Girls tend to develop acne on the face, while boys are more likely to get it on the chest and back. Washing with soap and warm water and putting medicated acne cream on pimples can help control these skin flare-ups.

Acne often develops in the T-zone of the face: chin, nose, and forehead. An oil-free moisturizer may reduce outbreaks.

◀ A CHANGING BODY

This teenage boy hopes to have the muscled body in the mirror. With puberty, he will grow taller and gain weight. His muscles will get bigger, and his shoulders will broaden. After puberty, he can lift larger weights. Until adolescents' bodies and bones mature, however, they should continue to lift small weights. Puberty brings a predictable sequence of events. For males, it usually begins with an increase in the size of the genitals. Then, hair grows in the pubic area and armpits, muscles get larger, the voice deepens, and facial hair grows.

Weight training can increase strength and help build strong bones. It is important to learn how to lift weights properly to avoid injury.

◀ SLEEP WELL

Why do so many teens seem to be wide-awake late at night? There may be a biological reason for this behavior. Scientists who study adolescents' sleep behavior think that the brain's internal sleep-wake clock resets itself during puberty. Instead of feeling sleepy at 9 or 10 P.M., teens are alert and unable to fall asleep. Because they must get up early for school, they do not get enough sleep. Researchers think teens need about 9 hours of sleep every night. On average, they get only about 7½ hours of sleep. Sleeping late on weekends can make up for some of this sleep loss, but a chronic lack of sleep can lead to poor grades, emotional problems, and physical health issues. So get your rest!

did you know? ....

THE PARTS OF YOUR BODY CAN GROW AT DIFFERENT RATES. YOUR HANDS AND FEET GROW FIRST, AND THEN YOUR ARMS AND LEGS. YOUR CHIN OR NOSE CAN EVEN GROW FASTER THAN THE REST OF YOUR FACE! DON'T WORRY THOUGH; THE REST OF YOUR BODY QUICKLY CATCHES UP.

QUARKS AND LEPTONS

What are you made of? You might think of bones, blood, skin, hair, or cells. But if you look closer, what are cells made of? For thousands of years, people have searched for the basic building blocks of matter. For the past 200 years, this search has focused on atoms and the particles that make up atoms: protons, neutrons, and electrons. Now, physicists think they have identified the fundamental particles—the smallest pieces of matter that explain what makes up the universe and what holds it together. Physicists have identified 6 types of particles called *quarks*, and 6 called *leptons*. An electron is one type of lepton. Protons and neutrons, however, are made up of quarks. Physicists have developed some interesting ways of describing the categories of quarks. The 6 quarks are one of 6 "flavors": up, down, top, bottom, charm, or strange. And each is further divided into one of 3 "colors": red, blue, or green. The discovery of quarks and leptons has posed many new questions and hypotheses for scientists to answer.

Stomach

▲ MUSCLE CELLS

Every living organism, including you, is made of cells. A human body is made of thousands of different types of cells working together. Within the stomach, for example, are muscle cells that work together, moving food through the digestive system. When these cells contract, they mash food and mix in enzymes that help break down larger molecules into smaller ones.

◄ MATTER EVERYWHERE

The girl and her tennis racket are both examples of matter. All living organisms and nonliving matter are made up of the fundamental particles called quarks and leptons.

▼ HOLDING THE CELL TOGETHER

A portion of the structure known as the cell membrane is shown below. The cell membrane separates the inside of the cell from its surroundings. The cell membrane holds the cell together and controls the movement of molecules into and out of the cell. A cell membrane is made up of molecules that include proteins and phospholipids. Phospholipids form a double layer, and they consist of groups of atoms that are arranged in shapes that look something like a head and two tails.

did you know? MOST COMMON MATTER CONSISTS OF UP QUARKS AND DOWN QUARKS, NOT THE OTHER 4 KINDS OF QUARKS.

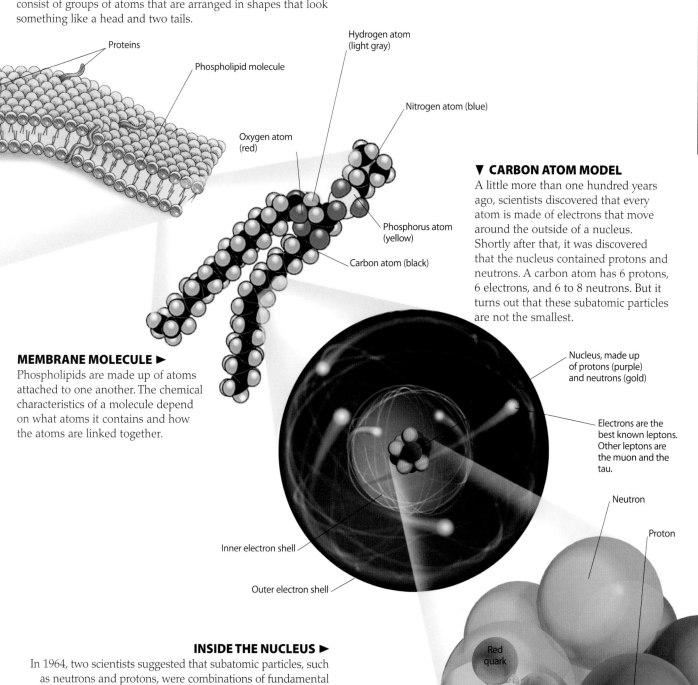

Proteins

Phospholipid molecule

Hydrogen atom (light gray)

Nitrogen atom (blue)

Oxygen atom (red)

Phosphorus atom (yellow)

Carbon atom (black)

MEMBRANE MOLECULE ▶
Phospholipids are made up of atoms attached to one another. The chemical characteristics of a molecule depend on what atoms it contains and how the atoms are linked together.

▼ CARBON ATOM MODEL
A little more than one hundred years ago, scientists discovered that every atom is made of electrons that move around the outside of a nucleus. Shortly after that, it was discovered that the nucleus contained protons and neutrons. A carbon atom has 6 protons, 6 electrons, and 6 to 8 neutrons. But it turns out that these subatomic particles are not the smallest.

Nucleus, made up of protons (purple) and neutrons (gold)

Electrons are the best known leptons. Other leptons are the muon and the tau.

Neutron

Proton

Inner electron shell

Outer electron shell

Red quark

Blue quark

Green quark

Naming quarks with color is just a way to identify different types. Quarks do not have color we can see.

INSIDE THE NUCLEUS ▶
In 1964, two scientists suggested that subatomic particles, such as neutrons and protons, were combinations of fundamental particles. They named these fundamental particles quarks. Since that time, experiments using large particle accelerators have shown that there are 6 kinds of quarks. Quarks are always found in groups of 2 or 3 that form a larger particle. Protons and neutrons are each made of 3 different quarks. Scientists hypothesize that at least one more fundamental particle exists and is just waiting to be discovered.

QUASARS

Quasars, first detected by radio signals in the late 1950s, look like stars but are gigantic, bright celestial objects that are really very far away. In fact, they can be 10 billion light-years away, close to the edge of the observable universe. The name *quasar* is an abbreviation for "quasi-stellar radio source." *Quasi* means "a resemblance to" and *stellar* means "star." They are called "quasi-stellar radio source" because they were first thought to be stars that were emitting radio waves. But as research advanced and telescopes became more powerful, astronomers discovered that quasars are actually active young galaxies with huge black holes at their centers. The amount of energy in quasars is hard to imagine. One quasar emits energy that is equivalent to 10 trillion suns! Astronomers think that black holes at the center of quasars swallow great amounts of matter, giving off enormous quantities of energy. That's why we can see their light. Studying quasars is essential for understanding how the universe was formed.

did you know?
....
BECAUSE QUASARS ARE BILLIONS OF LIGHT-YEARS AWAY, WHAT WE SEE TODAY THROUGH OUR TELESCOPES IS WHAT ACTUALLY HAPPENED IN THE UNIVERSE BILLIONS OF YEARS AGO.

THE BIRTH OF QUASARS ▶

Forming a quasar takes an incredible amount of mass and energy. Some quasars are formed when two or more galaxies merge. As they approach each other, their immense gravity pulls them toward each other. When they collide, a titanic explosion triggers the formation of new stars and materials. One result of two merging galaxies is that huge amounts of gases are pulled toward the central region, providing fuel for the black hole. The energy produced by the inflow of gases is so great that a quasar is formed. After this cataclysmic event, hundreds of millions of years will pass before the new quasar settles into a relatively quiet existence.

Many galaxies, including our own, have a black hole at the center.

When these two galaxies merge, a quasar will form. The energy produced by such a collision is extraordinary.

Matter gets pulled in toward a galaxy by the gravity of a super massive black hole.

A galaxy that gives off energy has an active galactic nucleus powered by a black hole.

▼ EVIDENCE OF COLLISIONS

The bright quasar in the center is 5 billion light-years away from Earth. But it has no host galaxy, which is a galaxy within which a quasar is embedded. Astronomers think the quasar is the result of a collision between a normal galaxy—one that is not active the way a quasar is—and an object that had a giant black hole. The cloudlike object above is probably a disturbed galaxy—one that has undergone a recent collision. The bright star below is nowhere near the quasar.

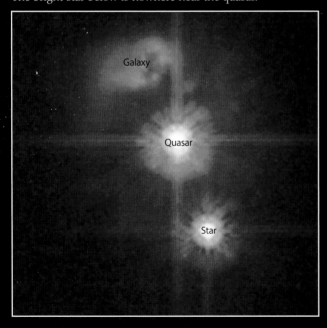

Galaxy

Quasar

Star

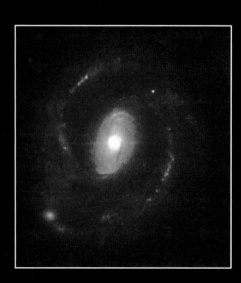

▲ QUASAR IN HOST GALAXY

A normal quasar like this one is surrounded by a host galaxy—in this case a spiral galaxy.

RACEHORSES

In the wild, helpful characteristics are passed on to the next generation of a species through the process of natural selection. But things work a little differently in the modern world. People can decide what variations they prefer in an animal and breed the animals with the goal of encouraging that trait. This process, called *artificial selection,* led to a breed of horse known as the Thoroughbred. All Thoroughbred horses are descended from three individual stallions (adult male horses) that lived in the early 1700s: the Darley Arabian, the Byerly Turk, and the Godolphin Arabian. The horses that run in famous races like the Kentucky Derby are Thoroughbreds. They have been bred to carry weight at constant speeds over long distances. However, their delicate leg bone structure can lead to serious injuries. If a horse is unable to distribute its weight evenly on all four legs, the swelling that may occur can be life-threatening. The horse racing and breeding industry in the United States is a big business. Thoroughbreds race for more than $1 billion in prize money every year. Top racehorse owners will pay more than $100,000 to mate their female with a certain stallion.

did you know?
....
A THOROUGHBRED'S HEART CAN PUMP UP TO 75 GALLONS (ALMOST 284 L) OF BLOOD PER MINUTE DURING A RACE.

SNOW RACING ▼
Every year in St. Moritz, Switzerland, Thoroughbreds race across not a dirt track, but a frozen lake. The snow-packed ice adds a new twist for horses and jockeys. Many of the same traits—speed, strength, and agility—that are desired in a Thoroughbred that races on a track are also important for a Thoroughbred that races on ice.

THE STEEPLECHASE ▶
The steeplechase is a horse race in which the horses are required to go over jumps. A race is between 2 and 4 miles long and includes 11 to 12 jumps. The traits of a good steeplechase horse are speed and precise jumping. If a horse cannot jump, it cannot win.

ANATOMY ▶

The height of a horse is measured in hands. A hand is 4 inches, about the same as the width of a man's hand. The average Thoroughbred measures 16 hands from the ground to the top of its shoulders, called the *withers*. Long legs and powerful muscles are desirable traits in a Thoroughbred.

Withers

A racehorse's power comes from its hindquarters, which should be muscular.

The Thoroughbred's eyes are set wide on its head. It can easily see the horses around it.

The Thoroughbred's back is shorter than the back of other breeds.

A Thoroughbred's long neck helps it keep its balance.

A galloping horse carries all of its body weight on the leading front leg.

RADIO

In a thunderstorm, you see the lightning before you hear the thunder, because sound travels much more slowly than light does. How does music travel at the speed of light to your radio? By riding on radio waves! Like visible light, radio waves are electromagnetic waves that travel at the speed of light. Radio waves can travel long distances without being scattered or absorbed. Radio stations transform sound waves into radio waves. They modulate, or change, the radio waves so that they represent the sound of speech and music. Those waves are transmitted from a radio tower. Radios in homes and cars receive the waves and convert them back into sound.

FM antenna

Side plate with holes for tuning and volume dials, external power source, and AM/FM selection.

Tuning dial

Back casing

AM antenna

Windup generator magnets

Windup generator coils

FREEPLAY RADIO ▶

The Freeplay radio was designed to work in places where electricity and batteries are not available. A solar panel on top converts the energy from visible light into electricity. Alternatively, you can turn the generator crank, which spins wire coils in a magnetic field to generate electricity. This electricity can be stored in the rechargeable batteries for later use.

TUNING IN ▶

Radio announcers, news broadcasters, and disc jockeys typically have all or some parts of the broadcast programmed onto computers. The radio station broadcasts its radio waves at a particular frequency, or number of waves per second. When you tune your radio to that frequency, you hear that station's music. For example, if you listen to WROK 93.1 FM, the signal from the station is transmitted at 93.1 MHz (megahertz or millions of cycles per second). When you select 93.1 on your radio, the radio is receiving only radio waves at a frequency of 93.1 MHz, and you can hear your favorite station. AM stations broadcast at lower frequencies that are measured in KHz (kilohertz, or thousands of cycles per second).

know? did you ....

FM RADIO IS BROADCAST ONLY AT FREQUENCIES OF 88 MHZ TO 108 MHZ. AM RADIO IS BROADCAST ONLY AT 530 KHZ TO 1700 KHZ.

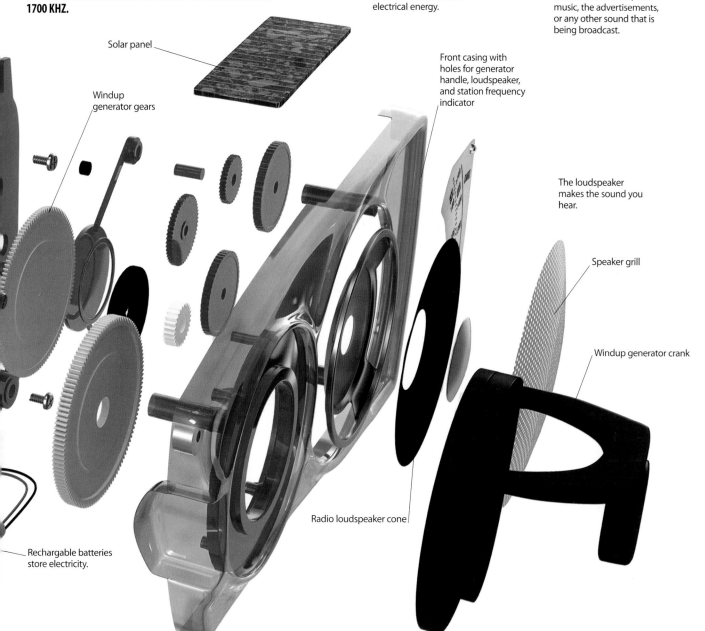

A microphone converts the sound waves of the broadcaster's voice into electrical energy.

The broadcaster uses the console to control the volume of her voice, the music, the advertisements, or any other sound that is being broadcast.

Solar panel

Windup generator gears

Front casing with holes for generator handle, loudspeaker, and station frequency indicator

The loudspeaker makes the sound you hear.

Speaker grill

Windup generator crank

Radio loudspeaker cone

Rechargable batteries store electricity.

RAINBOWS

Whether they form while you are washing the car or during a cloudburst, rainbows happen because of light energy interacting with matter. Rainbows form from sunlight that is both reflected and refracted by water droplets suspended in the atmosphere. To reflect means to bounce light, such as when light hits a mirror. To refract means to bend light. Instead of traveling along a straight path, a beam of light bends or moves off at an angle from the object it strikes. Refraction happens when white light strikes a prism or a raindrop. White light is made up of many colors of light, called *wavelengths*. A rainbow forms because water refracts the different wavelengths at slightly different angles and separates the colors. Violet light bends more than red light. The farther the light travels from where it refracts, the more spread out the colors of the rainbow appear in the sky.

◄ THE MAGIC NUMBER

Rainbows form when sunlight enters and leaves water droplets at a 42-degree angle. As long as that condition is met, even spray from a waterfall can form a rainbow. For this reason, the highest point at which a rainbow can form is at a 42-degree angle above the horizon. If the sun is higher than that, a rainbow cannot form.

A RAINBOW'S SHAPE AND COLOR ▲

Rainbows are arc-shaped because water droplets are round and the inside surface that reflects the light is curved. At sunset, rainbows are semicircular. When the sun is higher, the arc is smaller. A rainbow's color intensity is affected by the size of the water droplets. Large droplets produce bright, well-defined rainbows. Tiny droplets form overlapping color bands that appear almost white.

UNDERSTANDING ALL THE ANGLES ▼

Sunlight, in the form of white light, refracts as it passes from the atmosphere into a water droplet. When the light strikes the back of the droplet, it reflects at an angle, and then refracts again as it passes back out of the droplet. Different colors refract at different angles because they travel at different speeds when they pass through water. The sunlight separates into the visible color spectrum on their way out. Rainbows can form a complete circle, because a circular droplet creates a circular reflection—but the horizon cuts the circle in half.

Raindrop

Red light has the longest wavelength and violet light has the shortest.

did you
know?............................
BRIGHT MOONLIGHT CAN CAUSE A "MOONBOW," OR LUNAR RAINBOW. IT IS HARD TO SEE A MOONBOW'S COLORS, HOWEVER, BECAUSE THE REFRACTED LIGHT IS DIM.

RAIN FOREST

When you imagine a rain forest biome, do you picture a hot, humid jungle filled with colorful flowers and birds; noisy insects; and spectacular snakes, frogs, and mammals? You might think rain forests exist only in the tropics, near the equator—but they are on every continent except Antarctica. Our own Pacific coast, from northern California into Canada and Alaska, is home to the largest temperate rain forests. Rain forests are defined by temperature and rainfall. Tropical rain forests receive between 72 and 360 inches (about 183–914 cm) of rain a year and have temperatures of about 80°F (about 27°C) and higher. Temperate rain forests are cooler and average 60 to 200 inches (about 152–508 cm) of rain a year. The differences in rainfall and temperature create two distinctive rain forest biomes, each with its own structure and wildlife.

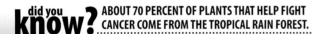

did you know? ABOUT 70 PERCENT OF PLANTS THAT HELP FIGHT CANCER COME FROM THE TROPICAL RAIN FOREST.

◄ **GOLDEN LION TAMARIN**
Weighing from 14 to 29 ounces (about 396–822 g), this species of small monkey lives in family groups in the canopy of Brazilian rain forests. For food, they depend on organisms and water inside certain plants, as well as fruit, insects, and small lizards. The golden lion tamarin is critically endangered because its habitat has been destroyed by deforestation.

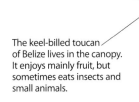

The keel-billed toucan of Belize lives in the canopy. It enjoys mainly fruit, but sometimes eats insects and small animals.

◄ GIANTS OF THE JUNGLE

Both tropical and temperate rain forests are divided into layers. Rain forests have an emergent layer, in which the tallest trees poke through the canopy. Growing to more than 200 feet (about 61 m), the trees of the tropical rain forest have ample space around them to spread their foliage. Between intense rainstorms, the emergent layer is exposed to extreme, drying sunlight and winds. The emergent trees of the temperate rain forest can grow to heights greater than 328 feet (100 m) due to their long lives—they usually live over 500 years!

ADAPTABLE ANIMALS ►

Tropical and temperate rain forest animals compete for food and shelter, so they must adapt to survive. Monkeys developed prehensile tails that can grasp branches. Other animals, such as this tree frog, sport bright colors to warn off predators or patterns to blend in with the forest. Still others have adapted a specialized diet and eat only one or two foods.

◄ THE FOREST ROOF

The dense branches and foliage of the tropical rain forest canopy shield the layers below from direct sun, wind, and heavy rain. Insects, birds, monkeys, snakes, and frogs feast on the abundance of fruits, flowers, leaves, seeds, and nectar. Fewer creatures live in the redwoods and other tall evergreen conifers—trees that produce cones and seeds—that dominate the temperate rain forest canopy.

Growing to more than 5 inches (13 cm) in length, the white-lipped tree frog of Australia is the largest tree frog in the world.

RAIN FOREST CONTINUED

Rain forests cover about 2 percent of Earth's surface, yet more than 50 percent of all plant and animal species live in them. Rain forests are a valuable, yet fragile, resource. They regulate global temperatures and weather patterns and help maintain Earth's limited supply of fresh water. Native cultures that live in tropical rain forests depend on resources from this environment for their survival. Valuable products, such as timber and coffee, are important exports, but they come at a price. Local and global companies with farming, timber, and ranching interests are deforesting the rain forest at an alarming rate. Although some deforestation is necessary to build homes and create agricultural areas, practices like clear-cutting and burning vast areas of land, as well as mining, are destructive. Rain forest destruction threatens biodiversity, promotes flooding, and causes soil erosion.

THE DARK MAZE ▶

Very little sunshine penetrates through to the understory layer of the tropical and temperate rain forest. Shade-loving plants with large leaves are home to insects such as beetles, bees, and ants. Snakes, lizards, and spiders can hide in the dense overgrown shrubbery.

JAGUAR ▼

Jaguars are fierce predators in the tropical rain forests of Central and South America. They hunt mainly on the ground, but sometimes pounce from tree limbs onto unsuspecting prey such as crocodiles, snakes, monkeys, and large piglike animals called *tapirs*. Jaguars are considered "near-threatened" because of deforestation and poaching.

The northern spotted owl is considered a threatened species. Its habitat has been severely reduced by logging of temperate rain forests in the United States and Canada.

Leafcutter ants bite off and carry away bits of leaves. They use the leaf bits to grow a fungus that they eat

LIFE IN THE UNDERSTORY ▶

Flowers in the tropical understory are large, pale, and heavily scented to attract pollinating insects. Many grow on tree trunks, unlike temperate rain forest flowers. Camouflaged reptiles and insects can easily hide from predators in the dim light.

◀ A SOFT LANDING

The soil of the temperate rain forest is rich and moist, covered with decaying needles and leaves. Wildflowers, grasses, mosses, and toadstools grow here. On the crowded floor of the Alaskan rain forest shown here, seeds can fall onto dead trees. Seedlings can take root right on the decaying trees, which are called *nurse logs*. The tropical rain forest floor is dark and the air is almost still. Little more than fungi and plants that get their nutrients from decaying leaves can grow in such darkness.

CREATURES OF THE FOREST FLOOR ▶

Termites, scorpions, and other invertebrates live on the tropical rain forest floor. Foragers hunt bugs and edible roots. Most temperate rain forest creatures live on or near the floor, where most of the food is. Chipmunks, birds, deer, black bears, and cougars are among these animals.

Its pattern helps the tropical Gaboon viper hide on the forest floor, waiting for its next meal.

did you know?..............
GABOON VIPERS HAVE THE LARGEST FANGS OF ALL SNAKES. THE FANGS CAN GROW AS LONG AS 2 INCHES (ABOUT 5 CM).

RATS

Unless you are someone who keeps a rat as a pet, you are probably among those who consider rats to be unwelcome pests. Rats can contaminate food, damage property, transmit parasites to animals and humans, and can carry infectious diseases. People find them in and around their homes and other buildings or in gardens and fields. Rats burrow beneath compost piles, build nests under wood stacks, and find their way into attics or garages. They climb, jump, and gnaw their way into places. They swim through sewers and enter through toilets or broken pipes. In areas where there is ample food, water, and shelter, rat populations can quickly grow into an infestation. Except for their eyesight, which is poor, rats have keen senses and can detect new obstacles in their environments. If they come upon a trap, for example, they will avoid it for days, making capture difficult.

Rats gnaw materials like paper, cardboard, wood, and upholstery and use the shreds to build nests.

DISEASE CARRIERS ▲

Rats are especially dangerous when they carry pathogens—bacteria or viruses—that cause food poisoning, ratbite fever, Lassa fever, and other infectious diseases. Infected rats carry the pathogens in their saliva, urine, and droppings. Disease is transmitted to humans through food and airborne dust that have been in contact with rat wastes, by direct contact with the animal or its wastes, and from bite wounds, which rarely occur. Scientists trap rats to collect information on the spread of a pathogen. The rat shown above will be studied to learn more about the virus that causes Lassa fever.

did you know?
WHEN RATS ARE FLUSHED DOWN THE TOILET, NOT ONLY DO THEY SURVIVE, BUT THEY CAN FOLLOW THE SAME ROUTE BACK TO THE BUILDING.

▼ KEEPING A LID ON RATS

Rats love rubbish—so storing garbage and animal feed in tightly sealed containers and fixing leaky pipes help reduce rats' food sources. Repairing building foundations and keeping property free of debris, junk piles, and old appliances limit shelter options. People generally use traps or rat poison to rid homes and buildings of rats. Poison, however, poses a safety issue in homes where children and pets live.

The Norway rat, also known as the brown or sewer rat, lives in urban areas on every continent except in Antarctica. These rats can measure up to 16 inches (400 mm) from nose to tail.

RECYCLING

In the United States, people create more than 250 million tons of garbage every year! About a third of that waste is paper. Plastics, food scraps, metal, and glass account for another third. The rest comes from yard trimmings, wood, textiles, leather, and rubber. Today, companies and individuals are taking steps to reduce waste. Many products contain less material than they used to. For example, 2-liter plastic drink bottles contain 25 percent less plastic than they did 30 years ago. Currently, there are more than 6,000 reuse centers in the United States, which collect and distribute items such as building materials, unused school supplies, second-hand clothing, and household goods. Finally, more and more of the products that companies manufacture use partially or totally recycled content. When we recycle, we use an existing product or material to create a new product or material.

did you know?
IT TAKES 8 TIMES MORE ENERGY TO MANUFACTURE A PLASTIC BOTTLE FROM NEW MATERIALS THAN IT DOES TO MAKE ONE FROM RECYCLED PLASTIC.

GET CREATIVE ▲
The container holding this plant was filled with yogurt when it came from the store. Reusing items eliminates the need to use raw or even recycled materials to create new items. Before you recycle an item, decide if you can find a new use for it.

GLASS ▶
Glass can be melted down to create other glass products, a process that uses much less energy than making new glass from quartz sand crystals. Glass can also be crushed and mixed with asphalt to create pavement for roads.

Aluminum and other metals can be recycled over and over again. Recycling just one aluminum can saves enough energy to run a television for 3 hours!

RECYCLED PAPER ▼
Paper and cardboard can be collected, de-inked, turned back into pulp, and bleached. Fibers break down when paper is recycled, so some new pulp must be added to the mixture to provide strength. Then new paper products such as these facial tissues are created. Unlike metal, paper can be recycled only 4–6 times.

Newspaper

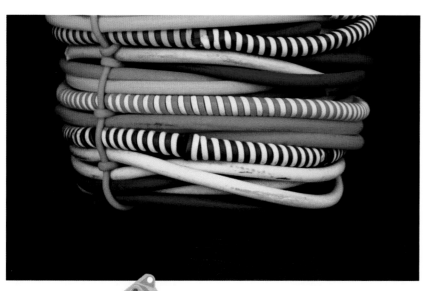

◄ TELEPHONE WIRE BRACELETS
In South Africa, women create colorful ankle bracelets from old telephone wires. When the women are finished wearing the ankle bracelets, the wires can be sent for recycling. The metal inside the plastic casings can be removed and used to create new products.

An old circuit board has found new life as a robot's eye.

The insides of an old toaster or tape player work just fine as a robot's body!

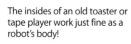

TECHNO-JUNK ►
Computers, cellphones, and other electronic products need to be discarded or recycled very carefully because they contain toxic materials that harm both people and the environment. In Europe, manufacturers pay the cost of recycling all electronic equipment they produce. The United States does not have such laws, but some nonprofit groups and some manufacturers provide "e-cycling" outlets for disposing of old electronic gear. A few states ban certain items, such as computer monitors, from landfills.

RED TIDE

Earth's waters are full of life—especially life that's invisible to the naked eye. This microscopic life includes unicellular algae that, in spite of their size, are hugely important to marine ecosystems. Like plants and some bacteria, many algae use sunlight and carbon dioxide to make their own food. Thus, they can form an important part of many food chains. However, too many algae can be a problem. When light, salt and nutrient levels, and temperature are just right, algae can multiply very quickly. Such a rapid increase in algae in an area is called a *harmful algal bloom* or *HAB*. These blooms, often called *red tides*, don't usually cause direct harm to humans. But a few types of algae release toxins that are poisonous to marine life and people. During these harmful algal blooms, it can be dangerous to eat certain catches of fish, because shellfish and fish that eat the algae become poisonous.

Flagella

▲ DINOFLAGELLATES CAN MAKE YOU SICK
Red tides are caused by dinoflagellates, which are plantlike protists. Protists are organisms that cannot be classified as animals, plants, or fungi. Dinoflagellates have two flagella. Flagella are tail-like structures that help a cell move. The cell can use one of the flagella as a whip to move it forward and the other as a rudder to steer. Fish and shellfish eat these organisms, and people or other animals that eat the seafood can become very ill. People can develop a severe stomachache and experience a tingling sensation in their fingers and toes.

◄ CRIMSON WAVES
Some species of algae cause the water to appear red when there are a lot of them. These algae are what put the "red" in red tide. However, not all algal blooms are red. Depending on the species that causes the bloom, a red tide can look red, brown, or yellow in color. Some algal blooms can even give off light. These bioluminescent algae can cause ocean water to glow at night.

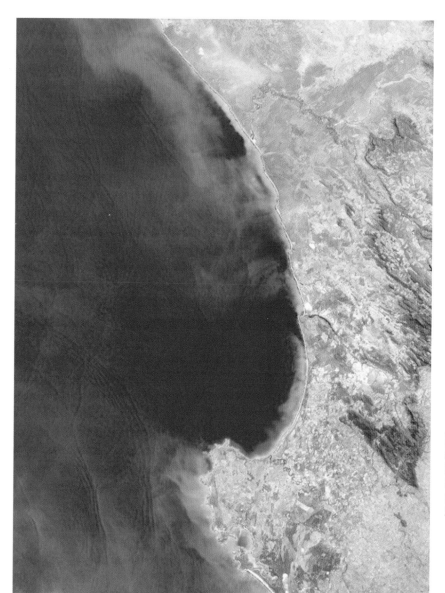

◄ SUFFOCATION OF WILDLIFE

As a large algal bloom decays, much of the oxygen that is dissolved in the ocean water is used up. The ocean water can have so little oxygen left that fish and other organisms suffocate. This red tide in Elands Bay, South Africa, caused 1,000 tons of rock lobsters to move toward the breaking surf in search of oxygen. They became stranded on shore when the tide retreated, and died due to lack of oxygen.

did you know?..

FLOATING MATS OF SCUM ON FRESH WATER MAY BE BLOOMS OF ORGANISMS CALLED *CYANOBACTERIA,* WHICH CAN HARM HUMANS AND ANIMALS.

POISONING A FOOD CHAIN ►

This sea lion pup has been orphaned due to the effects of a harmful algal bloom. When fish and shellfish eat the algae, they ingest dangerous amounts of poison. Sea lions and other animals that eat these poisoned fish get sick. In this way, a red tide can harm an entire food chain. HABs have harmed all types of creatures—anchovies, clams, mackerel, pelicans, loons, dolphins, manatees, and even whales.

REDWOODS

Gaze up into the limbs of a 100-foot (30-m) tall redwood and you get a glimpse of life 144 million years ago. Back when dinosaurs roamed Earth, redwoods grew across North America. But over time, as the climate changed, they declined. Today three species of redwoods inhabit Earth: coast redwoods, giant sequoias, and dawn redwoods. Coast redwoods populate a narrow strip of land about 450 miles (725 km) long that runs along the Pacific Coast. The tallest living tree is a coast redwood named Hyperion. At 379.1 feet (115.5 m) tall, it's nearly 74 feet (almost 23 m) taller than the Statue of Liberty! Giant sequoias are found in the Sierra Nevada mountain range of central California. The dawn redwood, native to China, is the smallest redwood, typically about 50 feet (15 m) tall.

TREE TUNNELS ▶

Years ago, tunnels were carved through some large redwoods so that people could drive through them! Fortunately, this did not kill the trees, because food and water travel through the outer layers of the stem. The heartwood at the center is inactive.

did you know?...............................

COAST REDWOODS CREATE THEIR OWN "RAIN" FROM FOG DRIFTING IN OFF THE OCEAN. THE FOG CONDENSES ON THE NEEDLELIKE LEAVES HIGH IN THE CROWN, AND THEN DRIPS TO THE GROUND WHERE THE ROOTS CAN GET IT.

◀ SHALLOW ROOTS

Redwoods have a shallow, fibrous root system that spreads laterally and to a depth of only 4–6 feet (about 1.2–1.8 m) below the surface of the soil. The roots can extend sideways as far as 125 feet (38.1 m) from the trunk of the tree. Roots of neighboring trees often become entangled, forming a strong network that supports all of them and helps them withstand heavy rain and wind.

COAST REDWOOD ▲

This tree has small, needlelike leaves and cones that produce millions of seeds no bigger than the seeds of a tomato. Redwoods also reproduce by cloning—new sprouts may grow up from a stump or the root system of a fallen tree.

GIANT SEQUOIA ▲

Shown here are the bluish-green leaves and seed cones of the giant sequoia. *Sequoia*, the name of a Cherokee man, is the genus name of both the coast redwoods and the giant sequoias. The common name redwoods comes from the reddish-brown color of the trees' bark and heartwood.

RENEWAL

Fires, floods, volcanoes, hurricanes, and other natural disasters and processes can disturb land and destroy living things. Renewal occurs when living things return after suffering from these events. Renewal can occur in two ways. Primary succession is a series of changes that occur in an area where no soil or organisms exist, such as the area around a volcano that has erupted. It is slow, often occurring over hundreds of years. Secondary succession is the series of changes that occur where land has been disturbed, but some soil and organisms remain. It can take more than a century for a forest to recover from a fire or human activity such as strip mining.

BURNING ▲
Small ground fires that occur every 50 to 100 years keep forests from becoming overgrown. Large wildfires can devastate a forest, as with this fire in Yellowstone National Park in 1988.

RECOVERING ▲
Although this area looks demolished, small patches of green plant growth indicate that renewal has begun. Recovery after a massive forest fire can take 100 to 150 years.

THE HEAT FROM GROUND FIRES POPS OPEN THE
CONES OF PINE AND SPRUCE TREES, RELEASING
MILLIONS OF SEEDS.

PLANTS GROWING IN LAVA ▼

Lava cools into nothing but solid rock. Most plants and
animals need soil to survive. Over time, weathering may cause
a thin layer of soil to appear. Then mosses and ferns grow. As
these plants die, the dead plant matter makes still more soil.
More and more plants can live in the area. Insects and other
animals return. It can take hundreds of years for this new land
to become a mature community.

Ferns begin to grow
in a crack of a lava
field in Hawaii.

NEW GROWTH ▲

It will be many years before this forest is full of trees again. But some
grasses and animals have returned just one year later. Insects are
abundant.

RHEUMATOID ARTHRITIS

Do you have an older relative or friend who suffers from arthritis? Chances are the individual has osteoarthritis, a common form of arthritis that develops when cartilage that cushions the joints between bones breaks down. Another type of arthritis, rheumatoid arthritis (RA), is less common, but can affect people of all ages. RA is an autoimmune disease, an illness that occurs when the body's immune system confuses healthy tissue for a disease-causing organism, called a *pathogen*. Normally, when viruses, bacteria, molds, and other illness- or infection-causing pathogens attack your body, the body's inflammatory and immune responses fight back. When RA occurs, the immune system mistakes the synovium, a membrane that lines certain joint surfaces, for a pathogen. Lymphocytes, pathogen-fighting white blood cells, try to destroy the synovium (also called the *synovial membrane*), just as they would an illness or infection. Unlike osteoarthritis, RA can affect other parts of the body, including the lungs, mouth, and eyes. Medication, exercise, and surgery can relieve symptoms, but there is no cure.

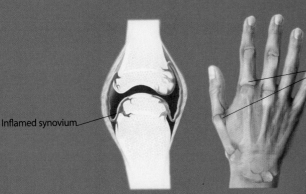

Inflamed synovium

Rheumatoid arthritis causes visible swelling of the fluid-filled cavities around several joints in this hand. Joints with cavities, or open areas, are called *synovial joints*.

THE IMMUNE RESPONSE ▶

If a pathogen gets into your body, your immune system fights back with two types of lymphocytes: T cells and B cells. Every pathogen carries a marker molecule called an *antigen*. T cells that recognize the antigen go to work, attacking damaged cells and activating B cells. B cells release proteins, called *antibodies*, that attach themselves to the antigens, marking the pathogens for destruction. In rheumatoid arthritis, T cells and B cells attack the body's own tissue.

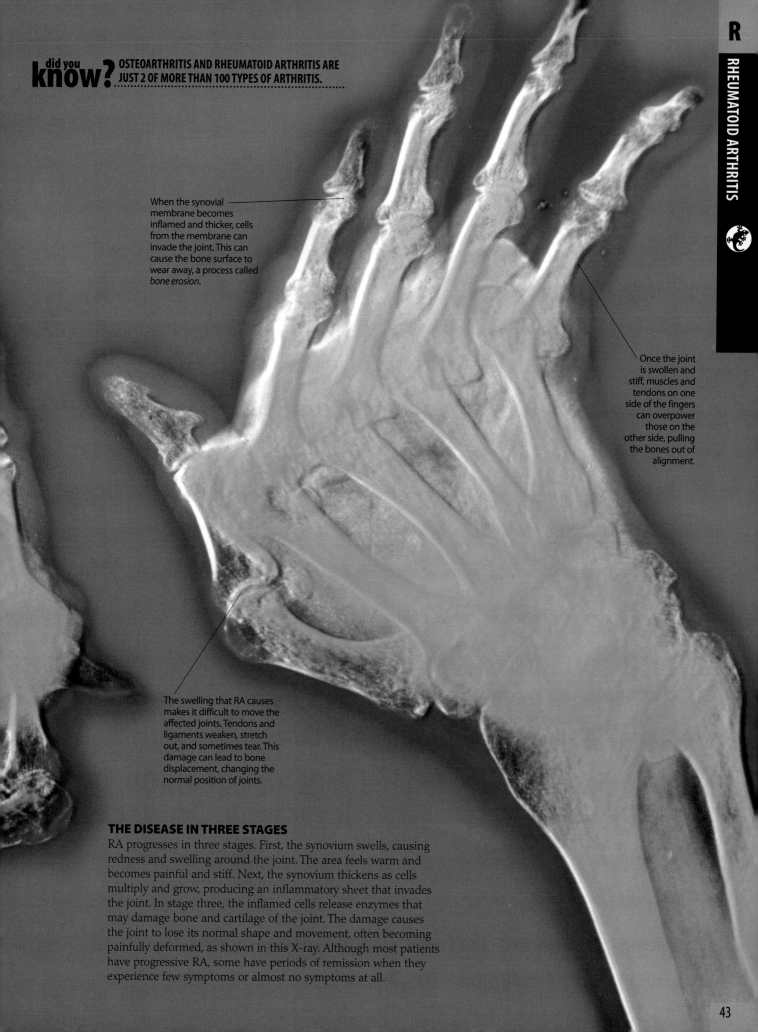

When the synovial membrane becomes inflamed and thicker, cells from the membrane can invade the joint. This can cause the bone surface to wear away, a process called *bone erosion*.

Once the joint is swollen and stiff, muscles and tendons on one side of the fingers can overpower those on the other side, pulling the bones out of alignment.

The swelling that RA causes makes it difficult to move the affected joints. Tendons and ligaments weaken, stretch out, and sometimes tear. This damage can lead to bone displacement, changing the normal position of joints.

THE DISEASE IN THREE STAGES

RA progresses in three stages. First, the synovium swells, causing redness and swelling around the joint. The area feels warm and becomes painful and stiff. Next, the synovium thickens as cells multiply and grow, producing an inflammatory sheet that invades the joint. In stage three, the inflamed cells release enzymes that may damage bone and cartilage of the joint. The damage causes the joint to lose its normal shape and movement, often becoming painfully deformed, as shown in this X-ray. Although most patients have progressive RA, some have periods of remission when they experience few symptoms or almost no symptoms at all.

ROBOTS

Would you let a robot operate on you? What if the robot were controlled by a surgeon? This may sound like science fiction, but robotic surgery is already being performed. In fact, robots are being used for many different tasks, with many benefits as well as some costs. Because robotic hands can be designed to be more flexible and steady than a person's hands, surgery can be performed very precisely through small openings in the skin. Surgeries performed this way have smaller chances of infection and shorter recovery times than standard surgeries. However, robotic surgical systems are extremely expensive. Robots are used for law enforcement, too. Their cameras can provide surveillance. Some police robots can detect hazardous substances or weapons. They can even move a bomb to a remote location for deactivation or harmless detonation. Robots are used in manufacturing as well. They may be able to turn out a product more quickly and cheaply than people can, but their use may lead to factory workers losing their jobs.

RECREATIONAL ROBOTS

Some robots are built for fun. For example, the two BRATs, short for Bipedal Robotic Articulating Transport, shown here can be programmed to perform different tasks, such as walking forward or backward, turning left or right, or moving faster or slower. They can even be made to identify an object like a ball, balance on one foot, and kick the ball. The BRAT can receive instructions through a computer cable, by remote control, or carry commands in its circuit board "brain."

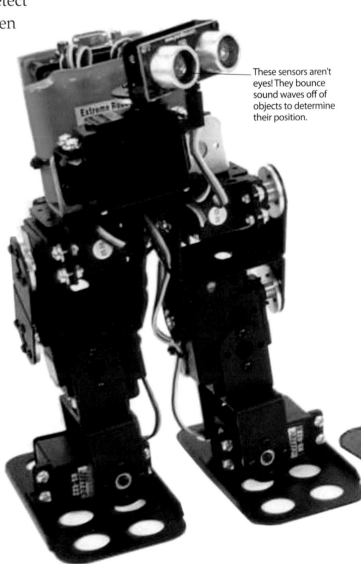

These sensors aren't eyes! They bounce sound waves off of objects to determine their position.

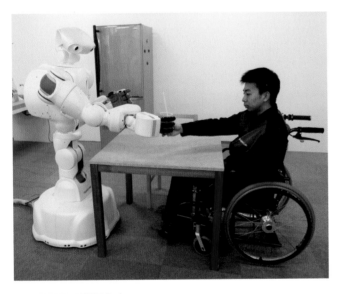

HELPING HANDS ▲

This robot, named "Twendy-One," is being developed in Japan as a helper for the elderly and disabled. Twendy-One is about 5 feet (1.5 m) tall and weighs about 245 pounds (111 kg). It can respond to human touch and is strong enough to support or carry a person. At the same time, its sensitive hands can safely pick up delicate objects without breaking them.

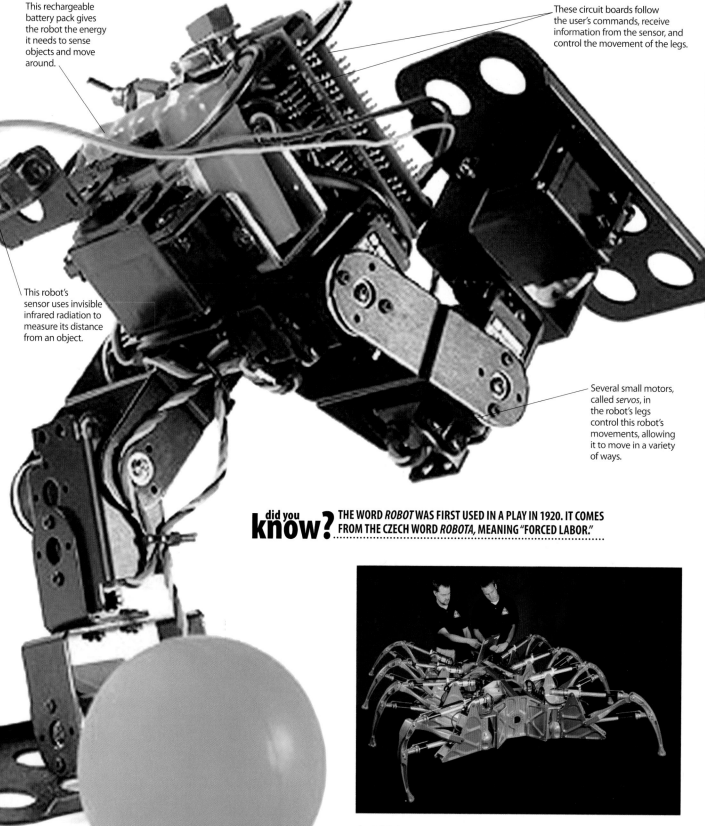

This rechargeable battery pack gives the robot the energy it needs to sense objects and move around.

These circuit boards follow the user's commands, receive information from the sensor, and control the movement of the legs.

This robot's sensor uses invisible infrared radiation to measure its distance from an object.

Several small motors, called *servos*, in the robot's legs control this robot's movements, allowing it to move in a variety of ways.

did you know? THE WORD *ROBOT* WAS FIRST USED IN A PLAY IN 1920. IT COMES FROM THE CZECH WORD *ROBOTA,* MEANING "FORCED LABOR." ....

▲ ROBOTS IN SPACE

Because of their size and fragility, future space vehicles will need to be built and maintained in space. However, space is not an easy place for humans to work. Enter Spidernaut, a robot designed to safely carry heavy objects while carefully crawling over delicate surfaces, such as solar panels or telescopes, while in space.

ROLLER COASTER

Clink, clink, clink. The roller coaster car slowly climbs its steep track. You grip the restraint in anticipation of a great fall. The thrills are about to begin! If you have ever been on a traditional roller coaster, you may have noticed that the cars do not have engines. They are pulled up to the highest point of the track by chains and then released. What causes them to go down and up again? Roller coasters can move along their tracks at great speeds because potential energy is converted to kinetic energy. Kinetic energy is the energy an object has due to its motion. Potential energy is energy related to an object's position or shape. In the case of a roller coaster, the potential energy is due to gravity and the height of the car. As the car falls, potential energy is converted to kinetic energy. The roller coaster car moves fastest at the bottom of a hill or a loop because all of the potential energy has changed to kinetic energy.

LOOP FORCES ▲

When a roller coaster car enters a loop, resistance to a change in motion, called *inertia*, keeps passengers in their seats. This continues as the car changes direction throughout the loop. When the passengers are completely upside down, the force of gravity acts on them, and they begin to fall. Luckily, the speed of the car keeps them moving in a circular path.

Roller coasters that go upside down may have a restraining bar that goes over the shoulders as well as the lap of the rider.

Steel roller coasters have tracks that are usually pairs of metal tubes. Wheels on either side keep the car firmly attached to the track.

HEIGHT VERSUS SPEED ▲

At the highest point on a track, the roller coaster car has all of its potential energy and no kinetic energy. It is completely still. As the car falls, its potential energy gets converted to kinetic energy, causing its speed to increase. At the bottom of the hill, the roller coaster car is going as fast as it can. The car has no more potential energy because its potential energy has all been converted to kinetic energy. The kinetic energy is converted to potential energy again as the car's momentum carries it up the next hill. Each hill or loop must be lower than the one before it, because some of the original potential energy is lost due to air resistance and friction between the car and its track. Engineers design the different heights along the roller coaster track carefully so that a car does not get stuck due to a lack of energy.

did you know?

THE FASTEST STEEL ROLLER COASTER IN THE WORLD, KINGDA KA IN JACKSON, NEW JERSEY, REACHES SPEEDS GREATER THAN 120 MILES (190 KM) PER HOUR.

RUBE GOLDBERG DEVICE

People would think you're crazy if you designed a complicated machine just to open up your closet. But that is exactly what Rube Goldberg liked to do. He was an engineer and a cartoonist intrigued by the way things work, and he had a great sense of humor. His cartoons showed complex and funny ways to complete a simple task. Instead of just flipping a switch to turn on a light, Rube Goldberg would draw a crazy machine with levers, pulleys, weights, ropes, ramps, balls, boots, and other devices to accomplish the task! His devices were compound machines. As you already know, a compound machine is composed of several simple machines, such as levers, pulleys, inclined planes, wedges, and screws. Rube Goldberg devices used many of these components. But in real life, machines are supposed to make work easier for people. They do this by changing the direction of a force, increasing a force, or increasing the distance a force is applied over. Instead Rube Goldberg machines made easy things difficult!

RUBE GOLDBERG COMPETITIONS ▼

Every year, high school and college students from around the country compete in local Rube Goldberg competitions. There is also a yearly national competition hosted by Purdue University in Indiana. Each year, there is an assigned task to be completed, such as squeezing an orange to make orange juice or peeling an apple. Using their imagination and scientific knowledge, students put together simple machines to build complex—and often funny— devices that perform the task.

did you know? ....

IN 2006, THE WINNING MACHINE IN THE RUBE GOLDBERG COMPETITION USED 215 STEPS TO SHRED FIVE SHEETS OF PAPER!

Simple machines, such as pulleys, are used frequently in Rube Goldberg devices.

▲ WHAT DOES IT TAKE TO CHANGE A LIGHT BULB?

During a Rube Goldberg Machine Contest®, the task was to replace an old-fashioned light bulb with a new energy-efficient bulb. Machines in the competition used weights, pulleys, cords, ramps, and balls. A Rube Goldberg machine is set in motion by an initial external force provided by a person. Then, every simple machine in the line is set off by the output force of the previous machine. Rube Goldberg machines illustrate the principle of conservation of energy, which states that the energy in a closed system remains constant but can change form. For instance, the potential energy stored in a resting ball changes to kinetic energy when it falls and triggers the next simple machine in a Rube Goldberg device.

A STRANGE "ALARM CLOCK" ▶

Rube Goldberg drew this crazy "alarm clock" cartoon. Would you like to be awakened like this? Check it out! The bird (A) catches the worm (B), pulling the string (C), which shoots the popgun (D), sending the cork (E) to burst the balloon (F). The dropping brick (G) depresses the bulb (H), causing the sprayer (I) to shoot perfume (J) on a sponge (K). As the sponge's weight increases, it pulls a string (L), which raises one end of a board (M). The heavy ball (N) rolls off the board, the string tied to it pulls out the cork (O), and ice water from the bottle (P) falls on the man's face.

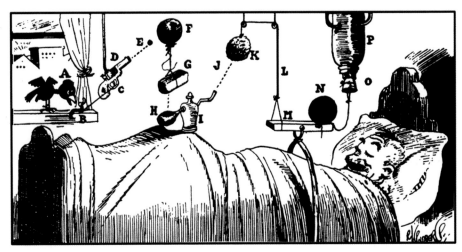

RUBIES

Whether blood red or pale pink in color, rubies are a special type of mineral called *corundum*. They are found mostly in a band of marble stretching 1,800 miles (about 2,900 km) along the southern slopes of the Himalaya Mountains. Geologists think that rubies were formed more than 60 million years ago, when two of Earth's plates converged and India began colliding with southern Asia. When this collision occurred, the limestone that formed the seabed was pushed deep down into the earth and was exposed to incredibly high temperatures—nearly 1,200°F (about 650°C)—and pressure of about 87,000 pounds per square inch (about 61 million kg/m^2)! The result of that process was marble. But that was just the beginning. Molten granite then found its way into the marble, removing the chemical silica from the marble and leaving aluminum and oxygen behind. As these aluminum oxides cooled, they formed crystals that are precious gemstones, such as rubies.

Ruby crystal

Marble rock with ruby crystals that have formed in it

Ruby crystal embedded in rock

This ruby crystal is still uncut. It is in its raw form.

DIFFERENT CUTS OF RUBIES ▼

In their natural form, rubies look like ordinary rocks. However, when cut into geometric shapes, they sparkle and shine with light. Rubies can be cut in facets, which are flat faces, or they can be polished to form round, smooth shapes. Different types of cuts, and different shapes in rubies, produce different effects of light. Rubies shine because light is refracted, or bent, and reflected from the cut surfaces.

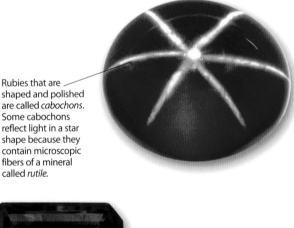

Rubies that are shaped and polished are called *cabochons*. Some cabochons reflect light in a star shape because they contain microscopic fibers of a mineral called *rutile*.

This synthetic ruby was not found in nature. Instead, it was made in a laboratory.

did you
know?...............
ONE OF THE LARGEST RUBIES IN THE WORLD IS MORE
THAN 5 INCHES (12.7 CM) WIDE. THAT'S LARGER THAN
THE DIAMETER OF A REGULAR SOFTBALL!

Scientists call all corundum that is not red a sapphire. But red and blue are not the only natural colors in these gems. Corundum also appears naturally as yellow, orange, pink, purple and other colors. All these hues are called simply "fancy color" sapphires to distinguish them from the classic red rubies and blue sapphires.

DIFFERENT COLORS OF CORUNDUM ▲

Although both rubies and sapphires are the mineral corundum, their color is different. Rubies are red or pink, and sapphires are blue or other colors. Corundum is a crystal made up of the elements aluminum and oxygen, and pure corundum has no color—it is called *colorless sapphire*. So why are rubies red? Because corundum can have impurities; in other words, small amounts of other elements are present in the gems. Rubies are corundum with chromium in it. Blue sapphires are corundum with titanium and iron in it.

RUBY MINES OF MOGOK ▶

Rubies are hard to find. A famous place where large rubies have been found is a mine in Mogok. Mogok is a region of Myanmar, an Asian country bordered by India, China, and Thailand. It has been exploited for these gems since at least the sixteenth century and continues to produce some of the most precious rubies in the world.

SAILING

Air is a fluid because it flows. And even though you can't see it, you can feel its power as wind. It can be strong enough to slow down an airplane, or to destroy buildings during hurricanes. But it can also be a great source of clean energy. For thousands of years, sailing was the best way to travel long distances. It began when people learned to harness the wind with small boats and simple sails, probably traveling close to the shores. Later, they ventured into the open ocean with larger boats and complex sails. They discovered global winds, which blow across long distances. Christopher Columbus used this method to cross the Atlantic Ocean almost 520 years ago.

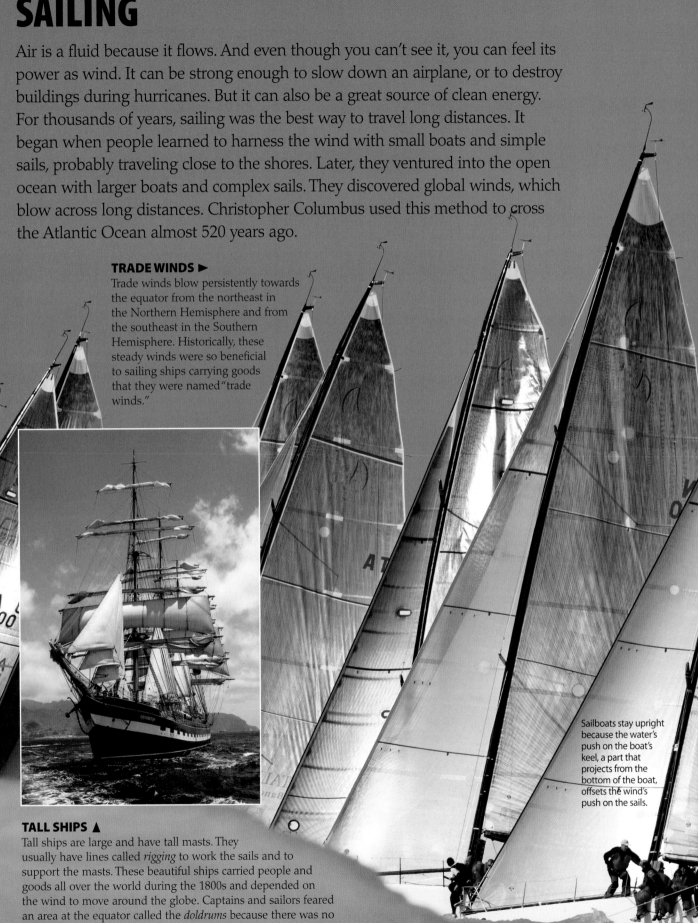

TRADE WINDS ▶
Trade winds blow persistently towards the equator from the northeast in the Northern Hemisphere and from the southeast in the Southern Hemisphere. Historically, these steady winds were so beneficial to sailing ships carrying goods that they were named "trade winds."

TALL SHIPS ▲
Tall ships are large and have tall masts. They usually have lines called *rigging* to work the sails and to support the masts. These beautiful ships carried people and goods all over the world during the 1800s and depended on the wind to move around the globe. Captains and sailors feared an area at the equator called the *doldrums* because there was no wind and ships could barely advance.

Sailboats stay upright because the water's push on the boat's keel, a part that projects from the bottom of the boat, offsets the wind's push on the sails.

◄ SAILING ON LOCAL WINDS

Some winds won't carry you across the ocean, just across the bay! These are called local winds because they travel over short distances. For example, a sea breeze is a local wind. Local winds form when Earth's surface heats unequally in small areas. Today, small sailboats like these take advantage of local winds for short-distance travel and leisure.

In some races, called *one-design races*, all the boats have the same design. The race measures the skill of the crew.

During a race, crew members have to dash from side to side to help keep the boat steady.

did you know?

A SAIL IN A SAILBOAT IS LIKE A WING ON A PLANE, JUST VERTICAL INSTEAD OF HORIZONTAL. IT APPLIES THE SAME PRINCIPLE OF COMBINING DIFFERENT PRESSURES TO CREATE LIFT THAT PROPELS THE BOAT FORWARD.

SATELLITE DISH

Have you ever wondered how we are able to watch an event such as an Olympics competition on television, as it takes place halfway around the world? A live telecast from so far away would be difficult without satellites and satellite dishes. A satellite dish is an antenna that receives and transmits electromagnetic waves relayed by a satellite. First, the light images and sound waves received by a television camera are transformed into microwaves. Then, those waves are beamed to a satellite and relayed to a television broadcast center. Next, they are beamed again via satellite to a local cable station or to a satellite dish at your home. Finally, electronics inside your television or a separate receiver box transform the signals back into images and sound. The whole process happens in less time than it takes to read this paragraph.

Radio receivers are attached to this platform that is suspended over the giant reflector. The receivers detect very faint radio signals reflected from the dish.

SOME DISH! ▶

The Arecibo Radio Telescope in Puerto Rico receives radio signals that are naturally emitted from stars, asteroids, planets, and other objects in space. The largest of its kind—1,000 feet (305 m) in diameter and 167 feet (51 m) deep—it can detect very faint waves. The dish reflects these signals into antennas that are suspended over the center of the bowl. In addition to picking up waves, the dish can also send out radar signals to study the surface of planets.

◀ RECEIVING SIGNALS AT HOME

Small satellite dishes, like the one attached to the balcony of the house to the left, receive signals from satellites that are orbiting Earth. The microwaves sent from the satellite hit the curved dish, which reflects and focuses the waves inward to a small device at the bottom of the dish, called the *feed horn*. A device inside the horn amplifies the signal, filters out radio noise (stray signals lacking content), and sends the signal via cable to the receiver inside the house.

4. A transponder inside the satellite boosts the signal so it is strong enough to return to Earth.

5. A transmitting antenna beams the signal back to Earth. The antenna can transmit to multiple destinations, including other satellites if necessary.

3. The receiving antenna collects the incoming microwave signal.

6. A downlink microwave signal travels back to Earth.

7. Ground station B receives the signal from the satellite.

2. An uplink microwave signal travels from Earth to a satellite.

1. Ground station A uses a huge dish antenna to beam a microwave signal to a satellite.

The 900-ton center platform is suspended 450 feet (137 m) above the dish by 18 steel cables, held up by three concrete towers.

Although this dish might look like a big lake, it is actually almost 40,000 perforated aluminum panels supported by cables suspended over a large sink hole. More than 16 football fields would fit in the dish.

TAKING AIM WITH A HIGH-FREQUENCY BEAM ▲

The waves that carry television signals are high-frequency waves called *microwaves*. They are the same kind of waves that can cook food, when concentrated in a small area. A television transmitter sends the waves out to a satellite as a narrow, focused beam. A signal composed of a narrow beam remains strong as it travels. It also can be aimed at a target, such as a satellite in orbit or a dish on the ground.

did you know?
NASA'S FIRST COMMUNICATIONS SATELLITES WERE 100-FOOT (ABOUT 30-M) MYLAR BALLOONS THAT COULD BE SEEN IN ORBIT WITH THE NAKED EYE.

About 700 B.C., the ancient Assyrians thought Saturn was a very brilliant star. For several centuries, people thought the object was a wandering star. In 1610, Italian astronomer Galileo Galilei viewed Saturn through a telescope. He was the first person to see Saturn's rings. The second-largest planet in our solar system, Saturn has a diameter of about 74,900 miles (about 120,540 km). That is almost ten times Earth's diameter. However, the planet is not solid like Earth. It is a large ball of gas with a solid inner core that is very hot—nearly 21,140°F (about 11,730°C). And, Saturn's atmosphere is very cold—close to –288°F (about –178°C). Saturn also has more than 61 moons. Some are very tiny, like Aegaeon, which measures about 0.3 miles (about 0.5 km). Others are huge, like Titan, which is bigger than the planet Mercury!

THE RINGS ▶

Saturn's most spectacular feature is its rings. These are made of billions of pieces of ice and rock that circle around the planet at different speeds and span about 175,000 miles (almost 282,000 km). Astronomers have now identified seven sets of rings, although not all are visible in this photo. Each set of rings is composed of many ringlets. Astronomers also think that these rings are the remnants of comets, asteroids, and moons that broke up and were captured by Saturn's gravitational pull.

did you know? SATURN IS ONE OF THE WINDIEST PLANETS IN OUR SOLAR SYSTEM. WINDS THERE CAN REACH 1,100 MILES PER HOUR (ABOUT 1,800 KM/H)!

Solar System

Mercury   Earth   Jupiter   Saturn   Uranus   Neptune

Venus   Mars

Sun

Saturn takes 29 Earth years to complete one orbit around the sun.

MOONS AND PROBES ▶

Scientists continue discovering more moons orbiting Saturn. Before NASA's Cassini-Huygens space probe was sent to Saturn in 1997, only 18 moons orbiting the planet had been identified, as shown here. Today, more than 61 have been discovered! NASA has sent four space probes to Saturn: Pioneer 11, Voyager 1, Voyager 2, and Cassini-Huygens, which arrived in 2004 and is still sending data back to Earth.

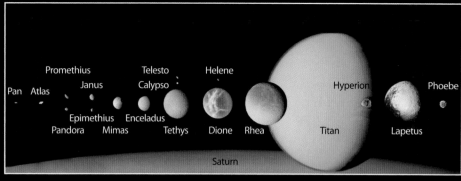

Pan Atlas Promethius Janus Telesto Calypso Helene Hyperion Phoebe

Epimethius Enceladus

Pandora Mimas Tethys Dione Rhea Titan Lapetus

Saturn

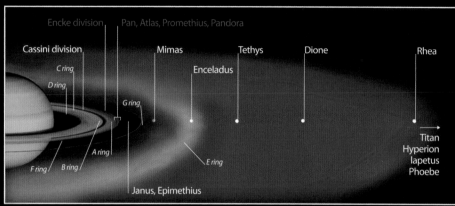

Encke division   Pan, Atlas, Promethius, Pandora

Cassini division   Mimas   Tethys   Dione   Rhea

C ring   Enceladus

D ring

G ring

A ring

F ring   B ring   E ring   Titan
Hyperion
Lapetus
Phoebe

Janus, Epimethius

The Cassini division is a space that separates Saturn's B and A rings.

Saturn's seven rings are named with the letters A through G in the order they were discovered. Looking outward from the planet, the rings are D, C, B, A, F, G, and E.

Saturn spins on its axis much faster than Earth does. A day on Saturn averages 10 Earth hours, 14 minutes.

SCENT POLLUTION

We can distinguish about 10,000 different smells. Smells can warn us of danger or make us start salivating. Some smells cause olfactory, or scent, pollution and may make us uneasy or sick. We are able to smell because of microscopic receptors high inside our noses and the process of diffusion. Diffusion occurs when odor molecules move from an area of high concentration—say, close to a baking cake—to an area of lower concentration. Because of kinetic energy, the molecules are in constant, random motion. They bump into each other, diffusing into the atmosphere as they move farther away from the source. Some of the molecules sweep up our noses when we breathe. With so many different odor molecules floating around, why are we not overwhelmed by smells? Our brains detect and process all the odor molecules around us, but register only strong odors or those we seek.

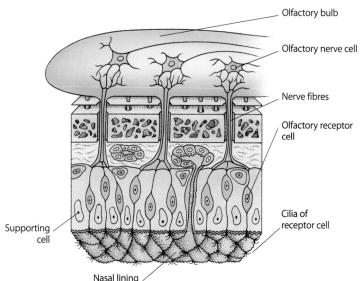

Olfactory bulb

Olfactory nerve cell

Nerve fibres

Olfactory receptor cell

Cilia of receptor cell

Supporting cell

Nasal lining

◄ SMELL RECEPTORS

More than 10 million olfactory receptor cells in our noses respond to odor molecules in the air. Each receptor has microscopic hairs called *cilia* that have smell receptors on the tips. When odor molecules stimulate the receptors, the receptors send electrical signals to olfactory nerve cells in the olfactory bulb. These cells then send signals to the brain where they are interpreted and identified as pleasant or unpleasant smells.

STEER CLEAR! ►

Many animals use scent to mark their territory or attract a mate. Skunks, however, spray an odorous oily stream or mist of scent in self-defense when they are attacked or threatened by predators. Most people think the mist is foul-smelling. At high concentrations, it causes nausea and irritates the eyes. Some people become violently ill. At lower concentrations, it may smell like rotten eggs, garlic, or burnt rubber. The human nose can detect skunk odors up to a mile away. Most predators avoid skunks unless no other food is available.

Not all animals have a nose to detect scent molecules. Moths have scent receptors on their antennae. Flies have receptors on their feet.

did you know?..............
OUR TONGUES DETECT FIVE TASTES: SWEET, SOUR, BITTER, SAVORY, AND SALTY. OUR NOSES DETECT THOUSANDS OF FLAVORS AND AROMAS, FROM THE STING OF A CHILI PEPPER TO THE NUTTINESS OF CHOCOLATE.

Because it takes ten days for a supply of smelly skunk spray to be made, skunks spray only as a last resort.

Today's perfumed soaps may contain more than 100 chemicals to make them smell like anything from strawberries to mint.

NOT SO SWEET

Fragrances in perfumes, colognes, soaps, other toiletries, and household cleaners are not as sweet as they smell. Most are made from toxic chemicals that can affect indoor air quality and harm people who have chemical sensitivities. The chemicals can trigger asthma, allergies, other respiratory problems, and headaches. They can cause dizziness and nausea and affect mood.

One perfume can contain hundreds of chemicals.

While humans have about 10 million smell receptors, bloodhounds have about 200 million.

SMELLS LIKE A ROSE ▶

Flowers release scent molecules to attract bees and other pollinators. Air pollution decreases the distance a flower's scent molecules can travel. One study showed that molecules that would have traveled 3,000 feet (914.4 m) in the 1800s might travel only 600 feet (about 183 m) today. As a result, bees have a harder time finding nectar for food, which may be one reason for the decline in bee populations.

SCIENCE AT WORK

Different types of scientists often work together. At the Woods Hole Oceanographic Institution® (WHOI), earth, life, and physical scientists team up to explore the ocean. Researchers work in the departments of applied ocean physics and engineering, biology, geology and geophysics, marine chemistry and geochemistry, and physical oceanography. They are assisted by Jason™, a remotely operated vehicle, or ROV. Jason is connected to a ship, where scientists can explore the deep ocean by viewing the live video that is captured by Jason's cameras. Jason is equipped with color video cameras, a sonar mapping device, robotic arms, and water samplers. Using these tools, Jason can collect organisms for marine biologists. It can also gather water and rock samples for ocean chemists. And it can use its sonar to scan underwater landforms for geologists. Jason can gather as much as 287 pounds (130 kg) of rock, soil, or living things. For moving larger amounts, Jason uses an "elevator." This machine is attached to a flotation device and can carry a large load up to the research ship while Jason keeps working.

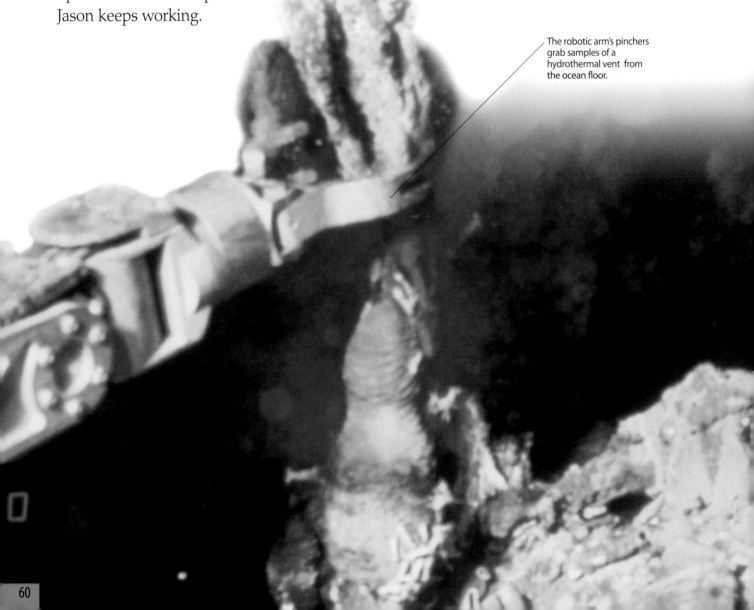

The robotic arm's pinchers grab samples of a hydrothermal vent from the ocean floor.

◄ JASON TAKES A DIVE

Jason has been so successful over its nearly two decades at sea that the first Jason (shown to the left) has been replaced by Jason II. Jason can now stay underwater for as long as 100 hours. It receives power through a thick, 6-mile (10-km) long cable that also sends live data and receives instructions through fiber-optic lines. The cable attaches to the research ship on the water's surface through a companion device called Medea™. Medea hovers no more than 115 feet (35 m) from Jason. It keeps the cable from yanking out while Jason explores. Medea also provides light for Jason and has cameras that give operators a bird's-eye view of Jason's work.

Jason and Medea are named for the adventurous ocean explorer of Greek mythology and for his wife.

did you know?

JASON'S TOP SPEED IS 1.7 MILES PER HOUR (ALMOST 2.8 KM/H). WHEN COLLECTING SAMPLES, IT MOVES MORE THAN 7 TIMES SLOWER.

▼ OBSERVING DEEP SEA WORLDS

To study rock formations, scientists collect samples from underwater worlds as deep as 4 miles (about 6.4 km) below sea level. It is important that Jason's instruments hold up under extreme pressures and temperatures. At hydrothermal vents on the seafloor, for example, boiling-hot, mineral-rich water and lava spew out from deep underground. Jason has also been used to rescue research instruments that have been trapped by chunks of hot lava.

CONTROL CENTER ▲

It takes at least six people to run Jason. The research ship to which Jason is attached must have a pilot, a navigator, and an engineer. In addition, three scientists must be onboard the research ship to run the control center. They use Jason's video cameras to help them collect data, steer the ROV, and control its robotic arms. Teams work in shifts for four hours at a time. In addition, scientists back on land receive and analyze data as Jason explores.

SCORPION

Scorpions are ancient, venomous arthropods that have existed for more than 400 million years! Found on all continents except Antarctica, scorpions most often live in deserts, although they have adapted to many different habitats, including forests and mountains. Like all arthropods, scorpions are invertebrates that are covered in a hard exoskeleton. As they grow, they shed, or molt, their exoskeletons and grow new ones. An interesting feature of scorpion exoskeletons is that they glow bright blue or green under ultraviolet light. Scientists are studying what advantages this may give scorpions, but it is still unknown. Scorpions have 4 pairs of legs, 6 to 12 eyes, and 2 claw-tipped arms called *pedipalps*. Their bodies are divided into 3 main parts: the head, abdomen, and tail. The tail ends in a stinging bulb called a *telson*. The telson is tipped with a sting that may be used to subdue prey before the pedipalps are used to eat it. Many scorpion species attack insects, spiders, and other scorpions as well as small mammals and reptiles.

did you know? SCORPIONS ARE RELATED TO EXTINCT SEA SCORPIONS THAT MAY HAVE BEEN MORE THAN 6 FEET (2 M) LONG.

TAILLESS WHIP SCORPION ▼

Despite their name, tailless whip scorpions are not really scorpions. Like scorpions and spiders, these wonderfully strange creatures are arachnids, but they belong to the order Amblypigi. Amblypigids have wide, flat bodies, and no tail. Unlike scorpions, tailless whip scorpions are not venomous. They capture and hold prey using a pair of pincers and tear the prey apart with sharp, slicing fangs (chelicerae).

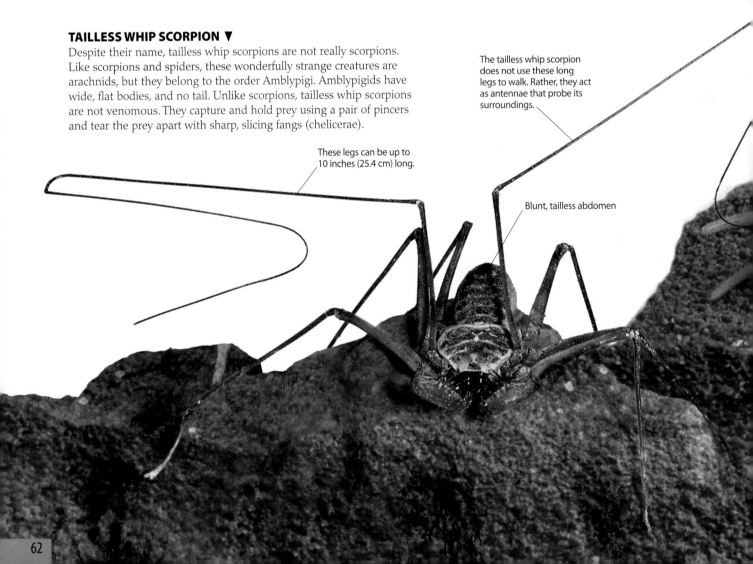

The tailless whip scorpion does not use these long legs to walk. Rather, they act as antennae that probe its surroundings.

These legs can be up to 10 inches (25.4 cm) long.

Blunt, tailless abdomen

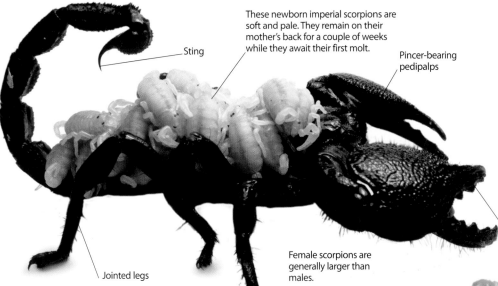

Sting

These newborn imperial scorpions are soft and pale. They remain on their mother's back for a couple of weeks while they await their first molt.

Pincer-bearing pedipalps

Jointed legs

Female scorpions are generally larger than males.

◄ **MOM AND BABIES**

Scorpions are viviparous, which means the females develop and nourish their eggs internally and then bear the young live. Eggs can take up to a year to develop into young scorpions. On average, females give birth to about 25 offspring. As the scorpions are born, the mother usually catches them in a basket she forms with her legs. The young scorpions then clamber onto their mother's back.

Some species use their claws to dig burrows.

DESERT HAIRY SCORPION ▼

The desert hairy scorpion lives in the deserts of the southwestern United States and Mexico. Reaching lengths of 6 inches (about 15 cm), this scorpion is the largest in North America. Despite its size and painful sting, the desert hairy scorpion has relatively mild venom. These scorpions are called "hairy" scorpions because they are covered in small brown bristles that detect vibrations in the environment. These tiny motion detectors help the scorpion locate prey.

The bulbous telson contains a poison gland that produces venom to stun and kill prey.

SEA HORSE

They probably don't look much like fish, with their horse-shaped heads; grasping, monkeylike tails; and kangaroo-like pouches, but sea horses are in fact fish. Around 32 species of sea horse live in shallow, coastal tropical and temperate oceans all around the world. These beautiful animals belong to a unique family of fish in which the male carries the fertilized eggs in a pouch and bears the young! They are the only animals known to reproduce in this way. Most sea horse species are also monogamous, which means that they mate with only one sea horse at a time. Males and females form mating partnerships that can last many years. To strengthen these bonds, sea horse mates often dance together and perform daily greetings. In addition to their unusual reproductive behavior, sea horses have other odd traits. For example, they don't have a stomach! The tiny crustaceans that sea horses eat go right through the animal's digestive system. This means that they have to eat constantly to avoid starvation. In fact, they can eat more than 3,000 brine shrimp a day!

did you know? THE FLESHY, CROWNLIKE KNOB ON THE TOP OF A SEA HORSE'S HEAD IS CALLED A *CORONET*. JUST LIKE HUMAN THUMBPRINTS, EACH SEA HORSE CORONET IS UNIQUE.

▼ SPINY SEA HORSE
The spiny sea horse gets its name from the sharp spikes that jut from its bony armor for protection. It lives in the coastal warm waters of the western Pacific Ocean, from Japan south to Indonesia. Like many sea horse species, spiny sea horses are commonly used in traditional and folk medicine in Asia, where they are thought to have healing properties. Unfortunately, such practices are hurting sea horse populations.

Courting sea horses entwine their tails together and dance in circles.

Sea horses suck tiny crustaceans through their snouts. They don't have teeth, so they have to swallow food whole.

◄ PREGNANT DADS

Male sea horses have a pouch in the front. The female deposits her eggs in this pouch and the male fertilizes them internally. He then carries the embryos until they are born about two weeks to a month later. Males can give birth to hundreds of babies. However, sea horse parents don't take care of their young. The little ones have to fend for themselves as soon as they are born!

Sea horse dads nourish their young in a womblike pouch located on the front of the body.

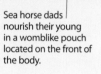

▼ SLOW MOTION

Unlike other fish, sea horses swim upright. They propel themselves along with a small, square dorsal fin located just above the tail. They steer using a pair of fins that stick out from the sides of their head like two floppy ears. Because sea horses are very slow swimmers,, they cannot escape predators by swimming away. Instead, camouflage helps to protect them.

Sea grass beds help hide this sea horse from predators.

Sea horse eyes move independently of each other. One eye can look up while the other looks down!

Sea horses don't have scales like other fish. Instead, they are ringed with bony plates armoring them against predators.

A prehensile tail allows sea horses to grasp things.

◄ YELLOW SEA HORSE

Yellow sea horses—also called spotted sea horses—are among the largest. Their thick, armored bodies can grow up to 6.7 inches (about 17 cm) long, and they have large, broad snouts to vacuum up tiny shrimp. Yellow sea horses are often bright yellow, but can also be dark brown or spotted. Like all sea horse species, a yellow sea horse's coloration changes to blend into the surroundings and as a way of communicating with another sea horse.

SEA STACKS

Water can't hurt rock, right? If you think that's true, think again! Powerful ocean waves can change the shape of seaside cliffs, producing amazing forms. Over millions of years, the constant pounding of ocean waves against these rocks has changed them dramatically. Erosion has worn them down and turned them into towers called *sea stacks*. The force of ocean waves erodes the softer, weaker rock, leaving behind the harder, erosion-resistant rock. And it's not only the force of waves that shapes the rocks, but also the sediments they carry—such as sand and gravel—and the power of the wind. When waves strike, the sediments scour the rocks. Over time, the sediment works the way sandpaper does on wood, wearing down the rock and creating new shapes. But sea stacks will not stand in the oceans forever. The permanent movement of the water will eventually erode them away.

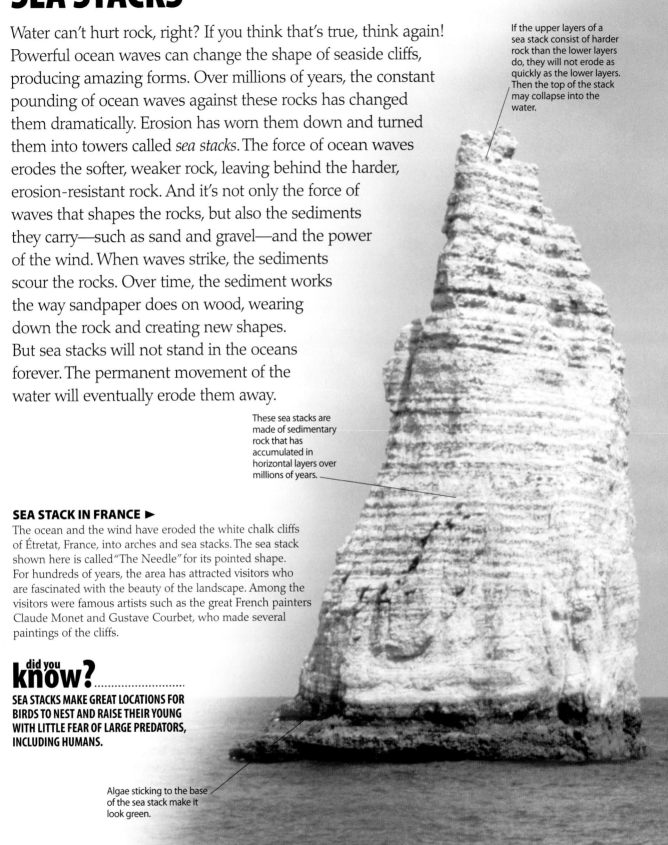

If the upper layers of a sea stack consist of harder rock than the lower layers do, they will not erode as quickly as the lower layers. Then the top of the stack may collapse into the water.

These sea stacks are made of sedimentary rock that has accumulated in horizontal layers over millions of years.

SEA STACK IN FRANCE ▶
The ocean and the wind have eroded the white chalk cliffs of Étretat, France, into arches and sea stacks. The sea stack shown here is called "The Needle" for its pointed shape. For hundreds of years, the area has attracted visitors who are fascinated with the beauty of the landscape. Among the visitors were famous artists such as the great French painters Claude Monet and Gustave Courbet, who made several paintings of the cliffs.

did you know?
SEA STACKS MAKE GREAT LOCATIONS FOR BIRDS TO NEST AND RAISE THEIR YOUNG WITH LITTLE FEAR OF LARGE PREDATORS, INCLUDING HUMANS.

Algae sticking to the base of the sea stack make it look green.

Waves moving toward the beach

Beach

Headland

Sea stacks

Arrows indicate the direction of wave distortion, or refraction.

The energy of wave refraction concentrates on the headland, causing erosion.

◄ THE FORMING OF SEA STACKS

Sea stacks form when the ocean's waves hit against a rocky coast. As the water becomes shallower near the beach, it encounters a high piece of land that juts outward, called a *headland*. The waves become distorted. This means that waves don't continue to move forward in a neat horizontal line. Instead, they curve following the shape of the seafloor. Scientists call this movement *refraction*, which causes most of the crevices and caves that form the sea stacks.

AUSTRALIA'S FAMOUS SEA STACKS ▲

The "Twelve Apostles" is one of Australia's most famous geological sites. These sea stacks formed as the ocean off Victoria, in southern Australia, wore away this limestone coast over the course of millions of years. They stand as tall as 147 feet (45 m). The Victoria coast is full of craggy headlands. That means that, eventually, more sea stacks will form.

SEA TURTLES

Sea turtles are found throughout the world's tropical and subtropical oceans. There are seven species of these marine reptiles, ranging from the relatively small Kemp's ridley to the enormous leatherback. Like other turtles, sea turtles are protected by a bony shell that has two parts: the carapace (top) and the plastron (bottom). Generally, the bony carapace is plated with hard scales called *scutes*, but the leatherback turtle has a flexible, ridged carapace covered in leathery skin. Most sea turtles are carnivorous. Different species eat different sea animals, such as sponges, jellyfish, crabs, and clams. Unfortunately, six of the seven species are threatened or endangered as a result of hunting and the destruction of nesting habitats.

GREEN TURTLES ▶

Green turtles are endangered sea turtles found in all of the world's temperate and tropical waters. They are the second-largest turtles in the sea, usually weighing 300–400 pounds (about 136–181 kg) and reaching lengths of 3–4 feet (about 0.9–1.2 m), although some have grown larger. Instead of munching on small sea animals, adult green turtles eat algae and sea grass, a diet that may contribute to their skin's greenish hue. However, juvenile green turtles are omnivorous and eat sea-dwelling invertebrates as well as plants.

Green sea turtles have been known to live more than 80 years in the wild.

did you know? UNLIKE OTHER TURTLES, SEA TURTLES CANNOT PULL THEIR LIMBS AND HEAD INTO THEIR SHELL.

The bony, beaklike jaw is toothless.

NEST MAKING ▼

Female sea turtles migrate from the sea to the shore to nest. The turtles swim to shore at night and crawl to a spot above the high tide line. Using their hind flippers, they dig nests in the sand and deposit clutches of 50–200 eggs. Finally, using their front flippers, the turtles cover the nest with sand to keep the eggs moist and to protect them from predators.

Front flipper claw

AT HOME IN THE WATER ▼

Sea turtles spend nearly all of their lives in the ocean but come onto land to nest. They are strong, graceful swimmers and top-notch divers. In fact, some species can dive more than 4,000 feet (more than 1,200 m) deep, and some can stay underwater for 10 hours! Sea turtles move easily through the water using strong, paddlelike front flippers. They steer using webbed, rudder-shaped feet.

Front flippers move in a figure-eight pattern.

Sea turtle shells are highly streamlined, which allows the animals to swim more quickly through the sea.

SEALS

Seals are carnivorous (animal-eating) aquatic mammals. Most seal species live in the world's oceans. There are two types of seals: eared seals and true seals. Eared seals, including sea lions, have small, external earflaps and long, flexible flippers that help them walk on land. True seals, such as the three types of seals shown here, have ears that are just tiny slits on the sides of their heads. And, unlike eared seals, they have shorter flippers and move around on land and ice typically by flopping forward on their bellies. In the water, however, all seals are agile and skillful hunters. Once they have captured their prey, they can swallow their food whole or tear it into chunks before swallowing. To conserve energy and extend their hunting time, at least two species of seals, grey seals and elephant seals, don't begin to digest their food until they have finished hunting.

SEAL DIET ▼

In general, seals eat mainly fish and squid, although diets vary by species, location, and season. For example, most of a crabeater seal's diet is made up of tiny shrimplike crustaceans, called *krill*. Hawaiian monk seals generally eat fish, spiny lobsters, eels, and octopuses, which live on or near the ocean floor. Northern elephant seals, living off the coast of California, eat squid and fish, as well as rays and small sharks.

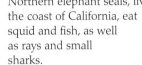

Krill

Squid

Cod

▲ **ELEPHANT SEAL**

This male elephant seal displays the feature for which these seals are named: an inflatable, trunklike nose. There are two species of elephant seals—northern and southern. Southern elephant seals are the world's largest seals. Males weigh up to 8,880 pounds (almost 4,000 kg) with a maximum length of over 20 feet (6 m). Great white sharks and killer whales are among their few natural predators.

▲ **MEALTIME**

Named for their spotted coats, leopard seals live in the bitterly cold waters off Antarctica and on a number of sub-Antarctic islands. Leopard seals are very aggressive predators. Their large heads, massive jaws, long teeth, and powerful flippers make them formidable hunters. Unlike other seals, leopard seals eat warmblooded prey, such as this penguin, seabirds, and other seals, in addition to fish and krill.

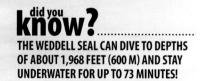

did you know?..................
THE WEDDELL SEAL CAN DIVE TO DEPTHS OF ABOUT 1,968 FEET (600 M) AND STAY UNDERWATER FOR UP TO 73 MINUTES!

▲ **A PUP'S FIRST FOOD**

This harp seal pup will nurse on its mother's milk for about two weeks. Her milk is so high in fat that the pup, which weighed about 24 pounds (11 kg) at birth, will weigh up to 88 pounds (41 kg) in two weeks' time. While nursing, this seal mother will not eat. She will live off the fat that she accumulated during her pregnancy. After the nursing period is over, the mother is ready to mate again, and she will leave the pup on its own. The pup will live off of its fat until it eventually learns to swim and hunt.

SEAWEED

Seaweeds grow in the sea but are not weeds. They are large algae. Most seaweeds cling to rocks or float along the beach in the zone between the low-water mark and the high-water mark. Some giant kelp species live deeper and grow into underwater forests almost 100 feet (30 m) tall. Other seaweeds float freely, forming vast living rafts on the surface. These floating clumps provide habitat for creatures found nowhere else in the ocean. Most seaweeds look similar to plants—some are classified as plants—but they have no roots, stems, or leaves. Like plants, seaweeds convert energy from sunlight into the materials needed for growth. Many marine animals rely on seaweeds for food and shelter, and some lay their eggs on them. Seaweed beds are important nursery areas for young fish. They provide a safe place to hide where food is usually in good supply.

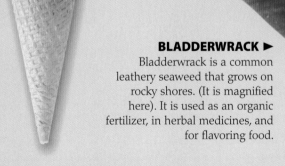

The blades contain pigments that absorb light and give seaweeds their color—usually green, brown, or red.

◄ SUSHI, PLEASE
In Japanese cooking, sheets of dried seaweed called *nori* are used in soups or to wrap sushi. Nori is full of vitamins and minerals such as calcium, zinc, iodine, and iron.

SEAWEED ICE CREAM ►
Seaweed extracts are used to jell, thicken, or stabilize many prepared foods. Dairy products such as ice cream and yogurt would be clumpy without them!

BLADDERWRACK ►
Bladderwrack is a common leathery seaweed that grows on rocky shores. (It is magnified here). It is used as an organic fertilizer, in herbal medicines, and for flavoring food.

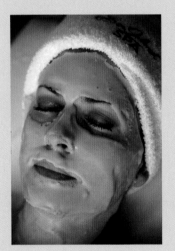

◄ GO GREEN
Seaweed is believed to nourish and detoxify the skin. It is a common ingredient in face masques.

◄ TOOTHPASTE TOO!
Seaweed is even used in toothpaste! A small amount of the substance called *carrageenan* from seaweed prevents the other ingredients from separating.

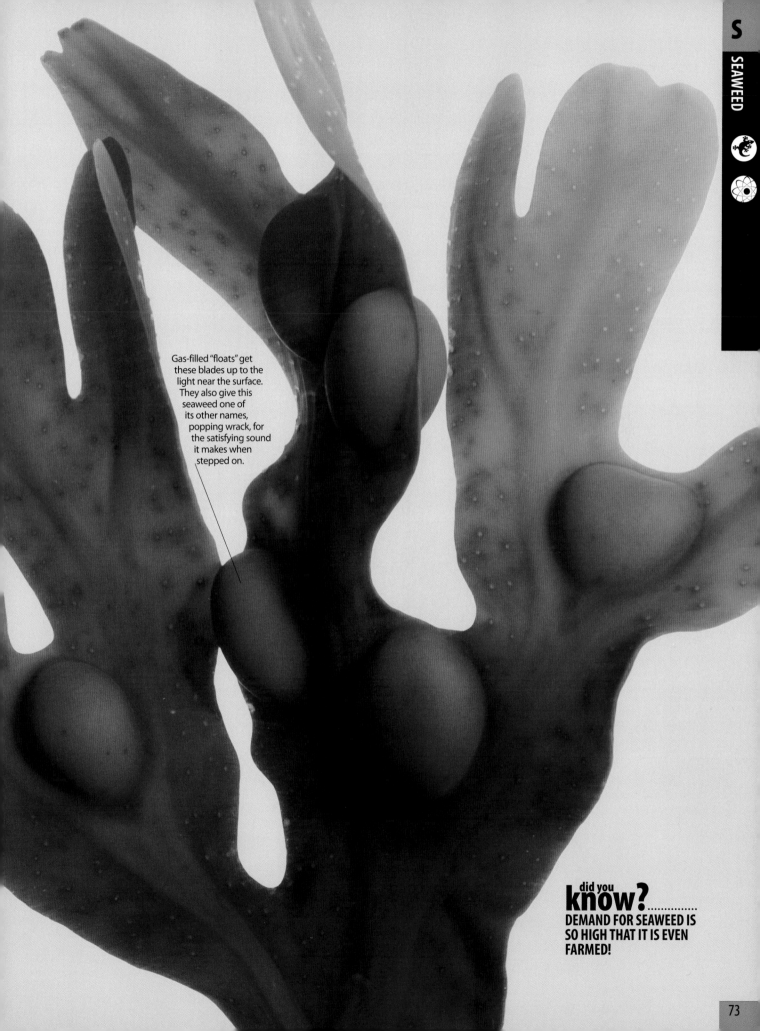

Gas-filled "floats" get these blades up to the light near the surface. They also give this seaweed one of its other names, popping wrack, for the satisfying sound it makes when stepped on.

did you
know?..............
DEMAND FOR SEAWEED IS
SO HIGH THAT IT IS EVEN
FARMED!

SEED BANK

In a vault on the Norwegian island of Spitsbergen near the North Pole sits a valuable treasure. It's not gold or diamonds, but seeds! The future of the world's food supply (and all other products we get from plants) rests with the seeds stored here in the Svalbard Global Seed Vault and in the more than 1,400 seed banks around the world. Each plant species may contain many varieties. For example, there are more than 100,000 different varieties of rice! Genetic differences within a species may mean differences in resistance to disease or in the ability to grow in different climates. At the same time, of the thousands of plant species that have historically appeared in peoples' diets, fewer than 150 are grown today. Plant species threatened with extinction due to natural disaster, disease, war, and climate change are helped by seed banks that maintain the diverse gene pools needed to feed the world.

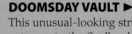

DOOMSDAY VAULT ▶
This unusual-looking structure is the entrance to the Svalbard Global Seed Vault. Nicknamed the "Doomsday Vault" and "Noah's Ark," it was built by the Norwegian government to provide a secure location for seed banks around the world to store duplicate collections. Its 3 storage chambers can hold a total of 4.5 million seed samples, each sample containing an average of 500 seeds.

INTERNATIONAL CENTER OF ▲ TROPICAL AGRICULTURE
The International Center of Tropical Agriculture (CIAT®) in Colombia holds the world's largest and most varied collection of beans, cassava, and tropical grasses from Latin America, Asia, Africa, and the Middle East. For more than 40 years, scientists and farmers have used these materials for research and agricultural purposes. The CIAT has already sent duplicates to the Svalbard vault for safekeeping.

▲ DEEP IN A FROZEN MOUNTAIN
The remote island location of the Svalbard Vault was selected in part because of its climate and geology. The deep underground location of the storage chambers in frozen ground will keep the vault's temperature cool enough to protect the seeds in case of a power failure. The facility's elevation—about 427 feet (130 meters) above sea level— will protect the seeds from any rise in sea level resulting from global warming.

did you know?
IN 2005, A 2,000-YEAR-OLD SEED FROM A NOW-EXTINCT SPECIES OF DATE PALM WAS SUCCESSFULLY SPROUTED, THE OLDEST KNOWN SUCH SPROUTING!

SHARKS

Sharks were here long before dinosaurs, and they haven't changed much in the last 100 million years. Sharks are "apex" predators, meaning they are at the top of the food chain. They help maintain the balance of their ocean environment by keeping the populations of prey animals from becoming too big. Often, they prey on sick and dying animals of many species. These include whales and seals, which have few predators because of their size. The shark population tends to increase or decrease in size as the size of its prey populations expand or shrink. However, the relationship between shark populations and their prey may be thrown out of balance due to overfishing by an unnatural predator of sharks—human beings.

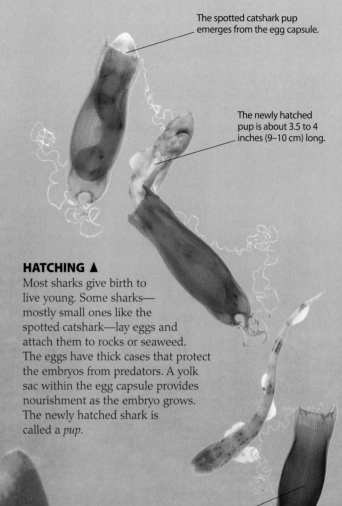

The spotted catshark pup emerges from the egg capsule.

The newly hatched pup is about 3.5 to 4 inches (9–10 cm) long.

HATCHING ▲

Most sharks give birth to live young. Some sharks—mostly small ones like the spotted catshark—lay eggs and attach them to rocks or seaweed. The eggs have thick cases that protect the embryos from predators. A yolk sac within the egg capsule provides nourishment as the embryo grows. The newly hatched shark is called a *pup*.

The egg capsule of the catshark and some other sharks is called a *mermaid's purse*.

KEEN SENSES ►

Sharks use some common senses such as vision, hearing, and smell. Other senses, such as electroreception and the lateral line—pores along the flank and back—are used mostly by aquatic animals. Electroreception makes sharks incredibly sensitive to electrical fields. This sensitivity allows sharks, like the oceanic whitetip shark shown here, to find hidden prey that can't be detected with their other senses. The lateral line system enables sharks to sense waves of pressure or disturbances in the water.

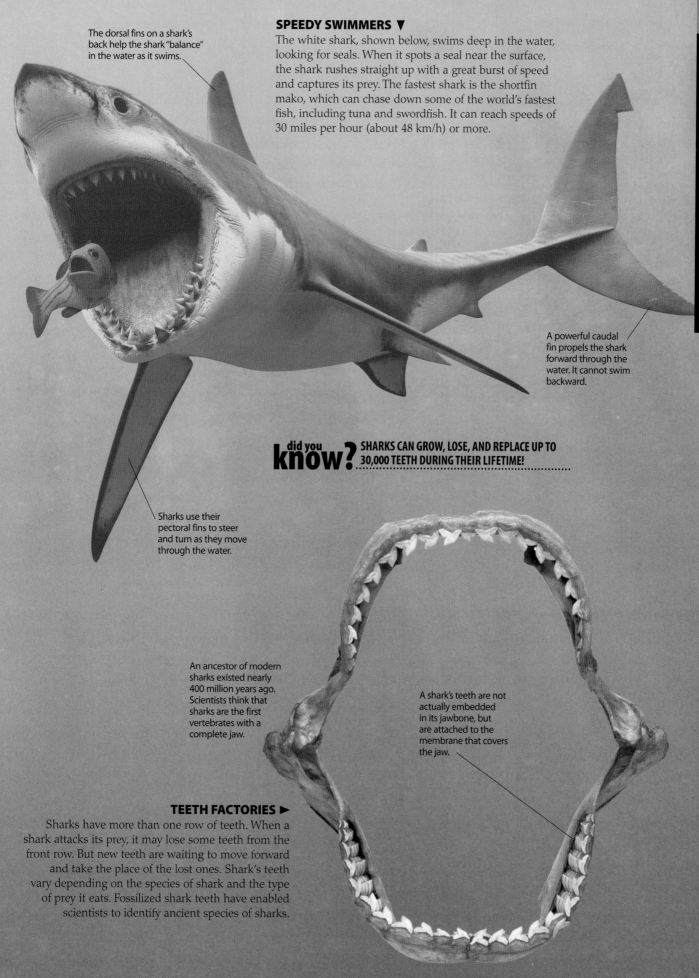

The dorsal fins on a shark's back help the shark "balance" in the water as it swims.

SPEEDY SWIMMERS ▼

The white shark, shown below, swims deep in the water, looking for seals. When it spots a seal near the surface, the shark rushes straight up with a great burst of speed and captures its prey. The fastest shark is the shortfin mako, which can chase down some of the world's fastest fish, including tuna and swordfish. It can reach speeds of 30 miles per hour (about 48 km/h) or more.

A powerful caudal fin propels the shark forward through the water. It cannot swim backward.

did you know? SHARKS CAN GROW, LOSE, AND REPLACE UP TO 30,000 TEETH DURING THEIR LIFETIME! ....

Sharks use their pectoral fins to steer and turn as they move through the water.

An ancestor of modern sharks existed nearly 400 million years ago. Scientists think that sharks are the first vertebrates with a complete jaw.

A shark's teeth are not actually embedded in its jawbone, but are attached to the membrane that covers the jaw.

TEETH FACTORIES ▶

Sharks have more than one row of teeth. When a shark attacks its prey, it may lose some teeth from the front row. But new teeth are waiting to move forward and take the place of the lost ones. Shark's teeth vary depending on the species of shark and the type of prey it eats. Fossilized shark teeth have enabled scientists to identify ancient species of sharks.

SHELTER

We have a basic need for shelter. From the beginning, people have built shelters to control their environments and to protect themselves from the climate, animals, and other people. These shelters have allowed humans to adapt to a variety of climates and live around the globe. Out of necessity, humans have been very inventive, using materials from their environment, such as snow, clay, wood, or reeds, to build shelters suited for their specific climate. Early shelters were very simple and not very durable. After the beginnings of agriculture, when people began to settle in one area for longer periods of time, shelters that lasted longer were constructed.

FLOATING HOMES ▶

These houses, and the islands on which they sit, float on the water of Lake Titicaca in the Andes Mountains in South America. Although the lake is 12,500 feet (3,810 m) above sea level, temperatures along the shore are moderate, around 46°F (8°C). Rainfall is 28–39 inches (700–1,000 mm) annually, and falls mostly during the summer. Both houses and islands are built from dried totora—a type of reed that grows in the marshes around the lake—by the Uru Indians. The islands rot from the bottom up, so new layers of totora must be added constantly.

These reed houses are typically one-room, simply constructed buildings with areas for cooking and sleeping.

BEDOUIN CAMP ▼

The Bedouin, animal herders who live in the Middle East, use tents for shelter when traveling in the desert. Despite the tents' dark color, the temperature is up to 15°F (8°C) cooler inside than outside, where temperatures frequently rise to 100°F (38°C). The loose weave of the tent cloth, made from goat's hair and sheep's wool, allows heat to escape. During rainstorms, the yarn swells. The swollen yarn combined with the natural oiliness of goat's hair make these tents almost waterproof.

The flat shape of the tent and long guide ropes prevent the tent from being blown away by the desert winds.

did you know?................

MATERIALS LIKE MUD, CLAY, AND STRAW ARE ONCE AGAIN BEING USED TO CONSTRUCT EARTH-FRIENDLY HOMES, IN PLACES SUCH AS THE SOUTHWESTERN UNITED STATES, MEXICO, AUSTRALIA, AND NEW ZEALAND.

PUEBLO ▲

Pueblos are permanent, multistory, connected homes built by, and named after, the Pueblo peoples of the American southwest. These community homes were traditionally built from adobe, a mixture of clay and water. The interiors stay cool during hot days and hold the sun's warmth during cool nights. The San Ildefonso Pueblo people have occupied this pueblo since sometime before 1300.

COOL SHELTER ▶

The Inuit people of Canada and Greenland sometimes live in temporary houses called *igloos*. Igloos are built from blocks of packed snow. While the outside temperature could be –40°F (–40°C), the temperature inside the igloo would be around 32°F (0°C).

Body heat slightly melts an igloo's walls. Once people leave the igloo, the walls freeze, better insulating the igloo.

In addition to providing transportation and food, camels provide hair that can be woven into cloth for clothing and shelter.

SIMULATORS

A strong wind catches the wing of your plane. You adjust the rudders and elevators, but you can't stop the spin. You're going down! That's okay; reset the machine and try a different response to the wind. By modeling lifelike conditions, flight simulators are great learning tools. Pilots can go through the motions of flight and see the results of their actions with no harmful consequences. A simulator is a machine that creates a model of a real-life situation, helping a student learn through touch, sight, and sound. Simulators can model technology, such as planes or trains, or environmental conditions, such as earthquakes. There are even robots that simulate the human body. Simulators can help golfers improve their swings. They help engineers test earthquake-proof structures and bridge designs. Pilots can practice flying new planes and dentists and doctors practice new procedures, all without any risk to others.

did you know? SOME TEENAGERS TAKE DRIVER'S TRAINING CLASSES USING A DRIVING SIMULATOR WITH REAL CONTROLS AND THREE COMPUTER SCREENS.

TRAIN SIMULATOR ▲

This man is operating a train simulator in Grand Central Terminal in New York City. Using the simulator, he can learn to safely handle dangerous situations such as fire, blocked lines, or snowstorms. New drivers can be trained using the simulator, and experienced drivers can learn new routes and practice using new controls when trains are remodeled.

Simroid's robotic parts are usually covered with human-looking silicone skin. Air-powered muscles allow it to move its face and hands.

Simroid is programmed to gag if a student pokes an instrument too far down its throat.

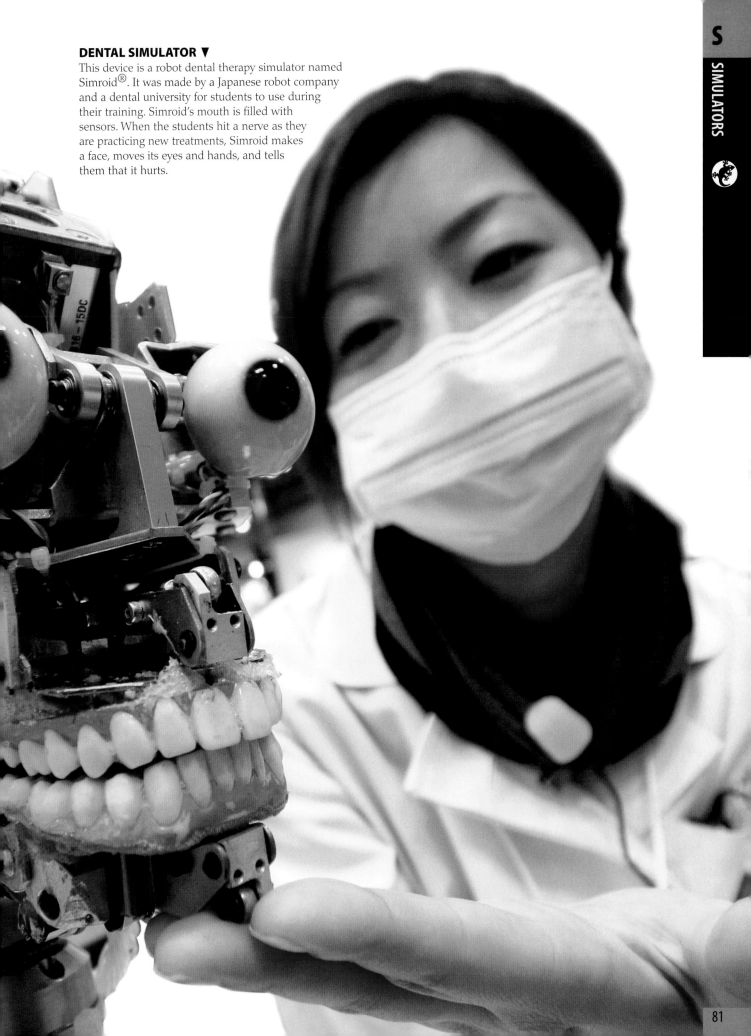

DENTAL SIMULATOR ▼
This device is a robot dental therapy simulator named Simroid®. It was made by a Japanese robot company and a dental university for students to use during their training. Simroid's mouth is filled with sensors. When the students hit a nerve as they are practicing new treatments, Simroid makes a face, moves its eyes and hands, and tells them that it hurts.

SINGING

You can do a lot of things with your voice. You can whisper, scream, and speak—and you can sing. When you sing, you use your voice to produce musical tones. But singing involves more than just your voice. Your lungs supply air, and your vocal cords—two folds of mucous membrane—produce the sound. The cavities in your chest and head amplify the sound. Everybody's singing voice is unique, because the shape and size of each person's vocal cords vary. The bone structure and tissues of the nose, throat, neck, and chest, and the size and shape of the mouth also vary. These factors each affect the tone, or quality, of the sound you produce with your voice, as well as its volume. The tongue, palate (roof), cheeks, and lips all contribute to the sound of the vowels and consonants you speak or sing.

A CHORUS OF VOICES ▶

The mix of voices in a chorus can produce beautiful sounds. Adult choruses are usually divided into four sections, based on singing pitch. Men's voices that are low in pitch are in the bass range. Higher male voices are called tenors. Women's (or young boys') voices in the lower range are called altos, and those that can reach high notes are sopranos. Women's and children's voices typically produce higher notes than men's, because their vocal cords are shorter and thinner and vibrate faster when air passes between them.

did you know?
HOARSENESS OR TEMPORARY DISAPPEARANCE OF YOUR VOICE IS OFTEN CAUSED BY SWOLLEN VOCAL CORDS THAT CANNOT VIBRATE PROPERLY, A CONDITION CALLED *LARYNGITIS*.

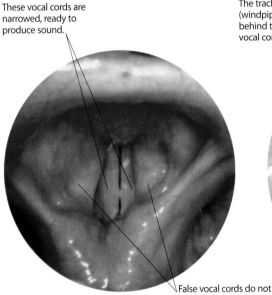

These vocal cords are narrowed, ready to produce sound.

False vocal cords do not produce sound; they help close the larynx (voice box) during swallowing.

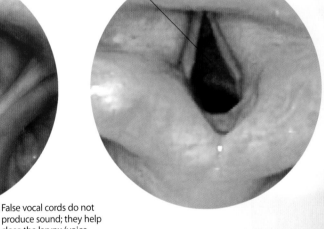

The trachea (windpipe) is visible behind these open vocal cords.

THE SOUND OF SINGING ▲

The vocal cords are located near the base of the larynx (voice box) and are attached by cartilages called *false vocal cords*. Tightening the muscles of the larynx pivots two of the cartilages, drawing the vocal cords closer together. Exhaling builds air pressure behind them. Air passing through the tightened vocal cords causes them to vibrate, producing sound. The tighter they are, the higher the note they produce.

THE SOUND OF SILENCE ▲

Although someone may ask you to stop talking, it would be just as effective to tell you to open your vocal cords. When the larynx muscles relax, the two cartilages pivot back, opening the vocal cords. In the open position, the vocal cords normally do not create sound. They allow you to breathe as air flows through the glottis, the V-shaped space between vocal cords.

A singer uses the tongue, lips, cheeks, and palate (the roof of the mouth) to form words with the sounds produced by the vocal cords.

SKELETONS

What words would you use to describe the word *bone*? Strong? Solid? Dead? If you said strong, you are right. Bones contain a fibrous protein called *collagen* that is combined with minerals such as calcium and phosphate. This nonliving material makes bones very strong and flexible. Solid? No. Most bones are made up of two types of bone: compact bone and spongy bone. While compact bone is very dense and firm, spongy bone is filled with small spaces that contain bone marrow. Dead? Definitely not. Most adult animals' bones contain a small percentage of living cells. Osteogenic cells, or bone stem cells, produce osteoblasts and osteoclasts. Osteoblasts make new bone tissue and eventually become osteocytes, which keep bone tissue healthy. Osteoclasts destroy damaged bone tissue, a necessary part of the bone repair process. Together, these cells allow bones to grow and to heal after injuries.

HUMAN SKELTON ►

The adult human skeleton is made up of 206 bones. The longest is the femur, or thigh bone. It is about one quarter of a person's height. The smallest, which is the stapes in the middle ear, is only a tenth of an inch (about 2.5 mm) long. However, when you are born, you have almost 300 bones. Some are made of cartilage, a strong, flexible tissue. Others are partly made of cartilage. Over time, these grow together and become the 206 bones in an adult.

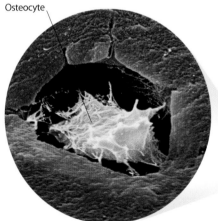

Osteocyte

Spongy bone

Compact bone

Femur

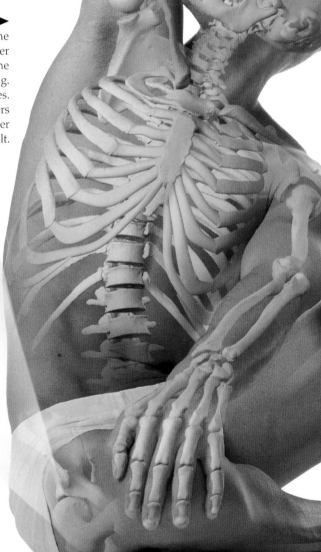

COMPACT BONE TISSUE ▲

Compact bone is made up of densely packed nonliving material that runs the length of the bone. Osteocytes are the cells that maintain the nonliving bone material by recycling calcium salts and assisting in repairs. They are located in small holes in the compact bone.

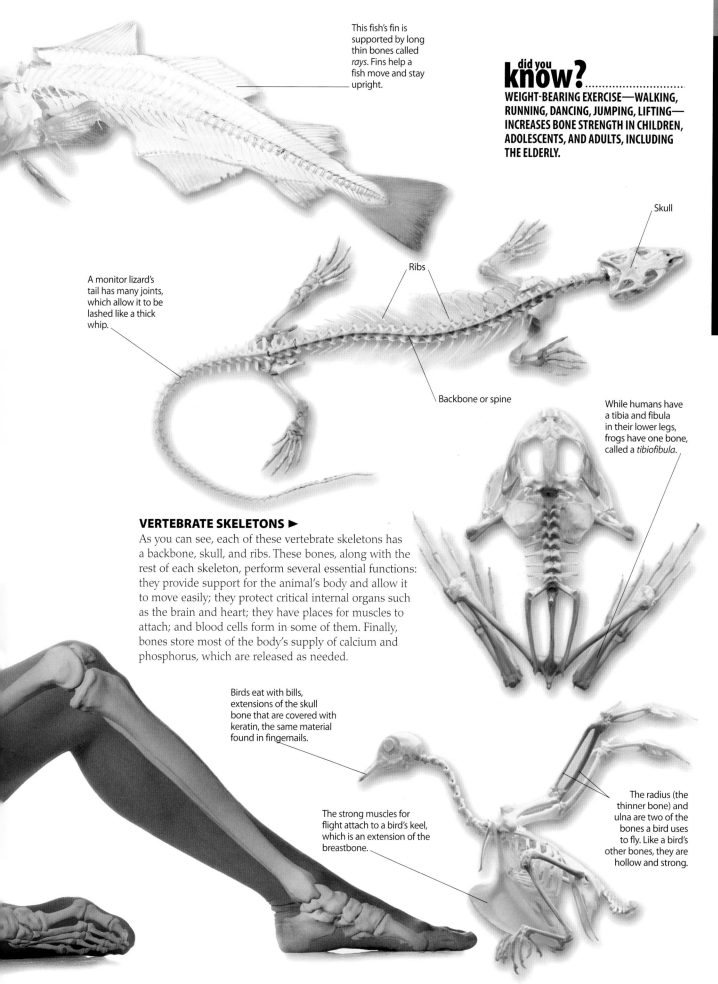

This fish's fin is supported by long thin bones called *rays*. Fins help a fish move and stay upright.

did you know?......................................
WEIGHT-BEARING EXERCISE—WALKING, RUNNING, DANCING, JUMPING, LIFTING— INCREASES BONE STRENGTH IN CHILDREN, ADOLESCENTS, AND ADULTS, INCLUDING THE ELDERLY.

Skull

Ribs

A monitor lizard's tail has many joints, which allow it to be lashed like a thick whip.

Backbone or spine

While humans have a tibia and fibula in their lower legs, frogs have one bone, called a *tibiofibula*.

VERTEBRATE SKELETONS ▶

As you can see, each of these vertebrate skeletons has a backbone, skull, and ribs. These bones, along with the rest of each skeleton, perform several essential functions: they provide support for the animal's body and allow it to move easily; they protect critical internal organs such as the brain and heart; they have places for muscles to attach; and blood cells form in some of them. Finally, bones store most of the body's supply of calcium and phosphorus, which are released as needed.

Birds eat with bills, extensions of the skull bone that are covered with keratin, the same material found in fingernails.

The strong muscles for flight attach to a bird's keel, which is an extension of the breastbone.

The radius (the thinner bone) and ulna are two of the bones a bird uses to fly. Like a bird's other bones, they are hollow and strong.

SKIN

The skin is the largest organ in the human body. Spread out, the skin of an average adult would cover about 22 square feet (2 m²). That's more than the average area of a front door of a house! The skin is more than a simple body covering. It is waterproof, keeping necessary fluids from escaping from the body. It is also a physical barrier to harmful substances, including infection by microorganisms. The skin is a sensory organ as well. It detects information in the environment—primarily temperature, pressure, and pain—and passes it on to the spinal cord and the brain. For example, the touch of a hot object on a finger produces pain. Nerves in the skin immediately send this information to the spinal cord. Nerve cells there trigger a response called a *reflex*: the automatic pulling back of the finger from the hot object.

did you know? A PERSON'S SKIN WEIGHS BETWEEN 6 AND 8 POUNDS (ABOUT 2.7–3.6 KG).

SUN DAMAGE ▼

Sunlight contains ultraviolet (UV) rays that can damage skin. The damage may be mild and temporary, like a mild sunburn. But over time, it can be serious and permanent. The most serious effect of sun damage is skin cancer. If not caught early, skin cancer, especially melanoma, is life threatening.

Sunscreens help protect the skin from ultraviolet rays. Doctors recommend using a sunscreen with a sun protection factor (SPF) of at least 15 on exposed skin.

▲ YOUNGER SKIN

Younger skin is much different from older skin. It is very flexible, elastic, free of wrinkles, moist, strong, and relatively thick. If it is protected from the sun, younger skin is generally free of damage caused by environmental factors. All this slowly changes as skin ages.

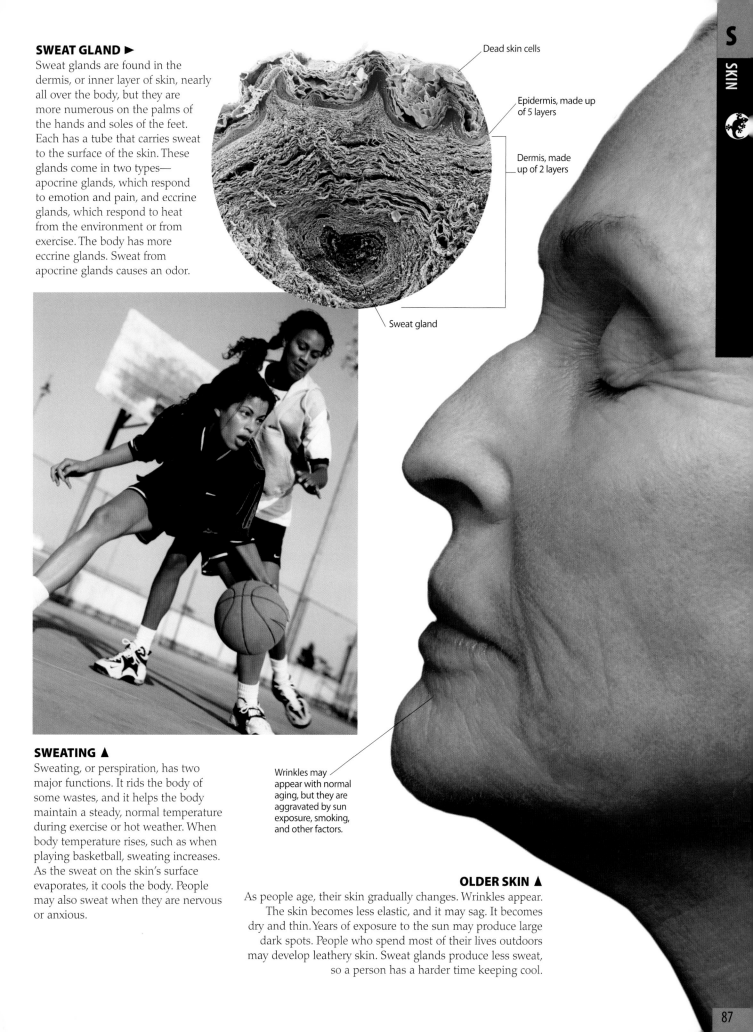

SWEAT GLAND ▶

Sweat glands are found in the dermis, or inner layer of skin, nearly all over the body, but they are more numerous on the palms of the hands and soles of the feet. Each has a tube that carries sweat to the surface of the skin. These glands come in two types—apocrine glands, which respond to emotion and pain, and eccrine glands, which respond to heat from the environment or from exercise. The body has more eccrine glands. Sweat from apocrine glands causes an odor.

Dead skin cells

Epidermis, made up of 5 layers

Dermis, made up of 2 layers

Sweat gland

SWEATING ▲

Sweating, or perspiration, has two major functions. It rids the body of some wastes, and it helps the body maintain a steady, normal temperature during exercise or hot weather. When body temperature rises, such as when playing basketball, sweating increases. As the sweat on the skin's surface evaporates, it cools the body. People may also sweat when they are nervous or anxious.

Wrinkles may appear with normal aging, but they are aggravated by sun exposure, smoking, and other factors.

OLDER SKIN ▲

As people age, their skin gradually changes. Wrinkles appear. The skin becomes less elastic, and it may sag. It becomes dry and thin. Years of exposure to the sun may produce large dark spots. People who spend most of their lives outdoors may develop leathery skin. Sweat glands produce less sweat, so a person has a harder time keeping cool.

SKYDIVING

As you take off in an airplane, you know that you are in motion. Your reference point, the airport, appears smaller and smaller as you move up and away. But if you think of the airplane as the reference point, you are not in motion. You maintain the same velocity—speed and direction—as the plane. If you skydive, on the other hand, your motion will be drastically different from that of the plane. As soon as you jump from the plane, the force of gravity will begin to accelerate you toward Earth's surface. Instead of moving forward with the plane, you are now watching the plane move away. The ground appears to be moving closer. When you open your parachute, your speed decreases suddenly. With about 5 to 7 minutes of parachute time, you can relax and enjoy the view, as you are ready for a safe landing.

To slow down, divers spread out their limbs to increase their surface area. In formation diving, several divers create shapes in midair.

FREE FALL

During free fall, an object accelerates, or falls faster, at the rate of gravity. Most skydivers experience between 45 and 60 seconds of free fall. Every second, a diver's velocity increases by about 32 feet per second (9.8 m/s). The diver continues to accelerate until the resistance of the air pushing up on the diver's body is equal to the force of gravity pulling down. The diver stops accelerating—but continues to fall at the same speed, somewhere around 124 miles per hour (about 200 km/h).

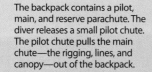

The backpack contains a pilot, main, and reserve parachute. The diver releases a small pilot chute. The pilot chute pulls the main chute—the rigging, lines, and canopy—out of the backpack.

Each skydiver wears an altimeter, a device that shows altitude. A reading in the red area of the dial indicates that the diver must open the parachute for a safe landing.

WHOOSH! ▲

Between 3,000 and 5,000 feet (914 and 1,524 m) above the ground, the diver opens the pilot parachute that pulls open the main parachute, a canopy made of nylon. The air presses up against the canopy, slowing the skydiver down enough to make a safe landing. If the main chute does not work, there is a reserve parachute. Many reserve chutes are automatically opened by a small computer. Even with the reserve chute, skydiving can be hazardous. Out of 2 million jumps made each year in the United States, about 30 people die.

SKYSCRAPERS

As modern cities expanded in the late 1800s, space for new buildings became scarce. The only place to go was up, and so the skyscraper was born. Improvements in the strength of steel and concrete made it possible to construct tall skeletons, or frames. These frames, rather than the walls, carry the weight of these tall buildings. Today, the tallest skyscrapers are more than 2,625 feet (more than 800 m) tall. Machines make the work of building skyscrapers possible. Complex machines that dig, pound, and lift are made up of simple machines such as levers, pulleys, and wheels and axles. For example, excavators dig holes for foundations using a lever to move a ton of dirt in one scoop. These simple machines can dramatically multiply the force that a person can exert. A worker in a crane may pull a lever that causes a pulley to lift a 1,000-pound beam hundreds of feet up.

THOUSANDS OF TOWERS ▼
This busy port on the island of Singapore in Southeast Asia has more than 4,000 skyscrapers. Chunks of steel or huge tanks of water inside the top floors of many buildings keep them from swaying too much in the wind.

The glass and steel exterior, called a *curtain wall*, doesn't support any of the skyscraper's weight.

To support a skyscraper's weight of 200 million pounds (about 90.7 million kg) or more, the foundation must sit on rock.

◀ **BRITAIN'S TALLEST**
Two new skyscrapers take shape near Britain's tallest building, the 50-story center tower at Canary Wharf in London, England. Cranes lifted about 30,000 tons of steel during the tower's construction. The elevator, another invention that uses the pulley, makes moving people and materials around the construction site easier.

The two buildings that flank London's tallest structure are only about 656 feet (200 m) tall. The Canary Wharf Tower, in the center, is 800 feet (about 244 m) tall.

▲ **BUILDING IN SHANGHAI**
Like many other Asian cities, Shanghai is experiencing a building boom. The tower crane seen in this picture is essential for building skyscrapers. For a large tower crane, lifting a half-ton beam is like picking up a toothpick; these cranes can lift 19 tons.

Skyscrapers built with more modern construction machines dwarf the Fullerton Building, which was Singapore's biggest building in 1928.

did you know?......................
THE LARGE AMOUNTS OF WATER THAT CONDENSE ON THE EXTERIOR OF A SKYSCRAPER CAN BE RECYCLED AND USED FOR FLUSHING TOILETS AND WATERING PLANTS.

SKYWALK

On March 20, 2007, people first walked on a glass pathway suspended 4,000 feet (1,219.2 m) over the floor of the Grand Canyon. Some hailed the Skywalk as an engineering marvel and a wonderful tourist attraction. Others, such as members of the Native American Hualapai tribe, were split over the Skywalk. The Skywalk was built on the Hualapai reservation, with the tribe's approval and requirement of low environmental impact. Some tribe members argued that the Skywalk would benefit the impoverished tribe by creating jobs and increasing its income from tourist fees. However, others felt that the land was sacred and should not become a tourist attraction. Environmentalists were concerned that development of the area around the Skywalk would destroy the natural beauty of the canyon. They also argued that an increase in visitors and cars would pollute the land and the air. Only time will tell whether its benefits will outweigh its costs.

Visitors can look out over the Grand Canyon through a glass wall that curves around the Skywalk.

Shock absorbers keep the Skywalk from bouncing up and down as visitors walk on its deck.

GLASS WALKWAY ►
The floor of the Skywalk is made of 46 transparent panes of glass, each weighing 1,200 pounds (544.3 kg). Each glass section is made up of 5 layers of 3-inch (7.6-cm) thick glass. This makes the deck of the Skywalk extremely strong, yet still allows visitors to look straight down into the canyon. People must wear yellow slippers over their shoes to keep the glass floor clean.

▼ THE STRUCTURE
The Skywalk is a horseshoe-shaped structure that is cantilevered, supported at only one end. It extends 70 feet (21.3 meters) out from the rim of the western edge of the Grand Canyon. Its steel and glass structure weighs 1.571 million pounds (almost 712,594 kg). It can support 71 million pounds (about 32.2 million kg) of weight, or about 71 completely loaded 747 jet airliners.

did you
know?...............................
THE FRAME OF SKYWALK IS ANCHORED DOWN INTO 46 FEET (ABOUT 14 M) OF THE GRAND CANYON'S BEDROCK.

The Skywalk's steel frame was built to withstand winds of 100 miles per hour (almost 161 km/h) and temperature changes that cause expansion and contraction.

SLEEP

No matter how big or small, all animals need to sleep. Just like food and water, sleep is necessary for survival. Without enough of it, we don't function as well, and our risk of developing diabetes and heart disease may increase. Each night, we cycle through five stages of sleep. At each stage, the brain's electrical activity produces different kinds of brain waves. In stage 1 sleep, you're just nodding off; your eye movements and muscle activity slow down. In stage 2, your eye movement stops and brain waves slow down. Stages 3 and 4 are called *deep sleep*. Your brain waves become extremely slow and it is difficult to wake up from these stages. The last stage of the cycle is called *rapid eye movement* (REM) sleep. During REM, brain activity, heart rate, and blood pressure all rise. REM is the stage when most dreams occur. As we sleep, nerve cells are repaired. We awake with our brains refreshed and ready for a new day!

Gorillas make nests to sleep in at night. They sleep for most of the night and take a nap in the afternoon.

did you know?
GIRAFFES SLEEP LESS THAN ANY OTHER MAMMAL, AVERAGING 30 MINUTES A DAY. THEY SLEEP STANDING UP AND WITH ONE EYE OPEN.

Lions sleep for 13 to 20 hours a day.

Chinchillas sleep during the day and are active at night.

Two-toed sloths sleep 15-18 hours a day. Like bats, they can cling to branches with their claws while fast asleep.

HIBERNATION

During the winter, finding enough food to survive can be a challenge. Some species of animals, such as chipmunks and groundhogs, have evolved so they miss winter altogether. They spend the cold weeks of the year in hibernation. When an animal is sleeping, its heartbeat and breathing slow down, and its body temperature drops. These changes are more dramatic during hibernation, which, unlike sleep, protects the body from cold temperatures.

Elephants may stand up for some of the 4-6 hours a day they sleep.

Horses can sleep standing up without toppling over because their legs lock in place.

Tigers can sleep for 16 or more hours.

Human babies need about 16 hours of sleep a day. Teens need about 9 hours and adults need about 8 hours.

House cats sleep up to 16 hours a day.

Pet dogs sleep for about 13 hours a day.

Hedgehogs hibernate in the winter and may enter a similar state, called *estivation*, in the summer.

SLOTH

A sloth is a tree-dwelling mammal about the size of a raccoon but much lighter in weight. Sloths spend much of their time hanging upside down in trees. Sloths can conserve energy for long periods of time, so they can get by eating mostly leaves, which are low in nutrition and energy. They don't have much muscle mass, so lightweight sloths can perch on thin branches to escape heavier predators. Sloths find all the food and water they need in trees. They are difficult for predators to spot because they stay very still most of the time. Although sloths are endothermic, their body temperature depends a great deal on the air temperature and fluctuates more than that of other mammals. Sloths have molars—peglike teeth that never stop growing—for grinding their food, but they have no front teeth. They use their lips to hold and tear leaves and plants.

THE UPSIDE-DOWN LIFE ▲
Because sloths spend most of their lives hanging upside down, their fur grows upside down, too. Most mammals have fur that grows toward the paws. But sloth fur grows away from the paws, so rain doesn't penetrate while they are upside down. Sloths are well suited for hanging. They cannot be easily dislodged when hanging from a tree. Staying in the trees contributes to their long lives (10–12 years in the wild), because they are most vulnerable to predators when they are on the ground.

did you know?..............................
ABOUT ONCE A WEEK, A SLOTH COMES DOWN OUT OF A TREE TO DEFECATE AT THE BASE OF THE TREE.

TWO TYPES OF SLOTH ▶
The descriptive names of two-toed and three-toed sloths refer to the toes on their front legs. All sloths have three toes on their hind legs. Two-toed sloths are nocturnal, while three-toed sloths may also be active during the day. Two-toed sloths eat leaves, fruits, and flowers. Three-toed sloths eat leaves from just a few types of trees. Although three-toed sloths spend most of their time resting and conserving energy, they sleep only about 9–10 hours per day. Two-toed sloths log 15–18 hours of sleep per day.

GREEN ALGAE ▶
Sloths have long hair, and each hair shaft has grooves in it. Green algae grow in these grooves, and can turn a sloth's hair a greenish color. Greenish hair helps the sloth blend in with the tree leaves. Hundreds of beetles may live on a single sloth and dine on its algae. Some moths also eat the algae on a sloth's fur.

The moist, tropical air in rain forests, where sloths live, is the perfect environment for algae to thrive.

Sloth claws are hooked and very strong. The claws help the sloth climb, defend itself, and hang upside down.

SLOTH MOTH ▲

The most common insect living on a sloth is a sloth moth. Not only do the moths feed on the sloth's algae, but they also lay eggs in the sloth's droppings. The larvae feed off the droppings, and when adult moths emerge from pupas, they fly up to find a sloth to live on.

A sloth can take a month to digest the leaves it eats. Nearly one third of a sloth's weight is the food in its many-chambered stomach.

A sloth's back legs are so weak that it cannot walk. On the ground, a sloth crawls on its belly by dragging itself with its front claws.

Sloths control their body temperature by moving into sunny or shady areas as needed, despite being endothermic.

A sloth's average ground speed is only 6 to 8 feet (about 1.8 to 2.4 m) per minute, which makes it the slowest mammal on Earth.

SNAKES

They're scaly, and they're slithery, and, compared with humans, they certainly are bendy. How far can humans bend backward? Trained performers can touch their heads to their rear ends. Now imagine curving so far that your backbone makes a complete loop. Human spines just can't do that, but a snake can twist its spine into many loops. And yet, people and snakes have something in common: we are both vertebrates, animals with backbones. Snakes are carnivores: they eat other animals. There are three methods that different snakes use to kill their prey. Garter snakes swallow live animals. Vipers use venom to kill their prey. And boas and pythons use constriction: they loop themselves around their prey and squeeze tightly until their opponent is dead.

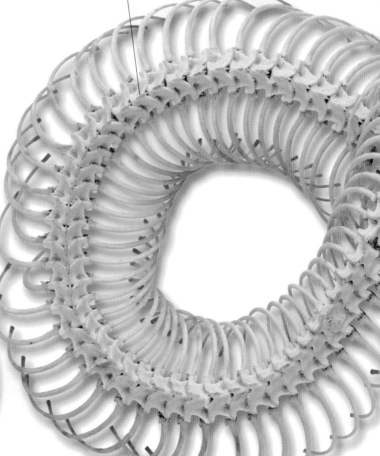

A python can open its jaw wide enough to swallow a goat or even a human.

A python can have as many as 600 vertebrae. Humans have only 24.

▼ THE SOFT PARTS

A Burmese python's eggs travel through the oviduct. Snakes have one hole, called the *cloaca*, for moving everything out their backsides. This opening is used for feces, urine, sperm in the male, and eggs in the female.

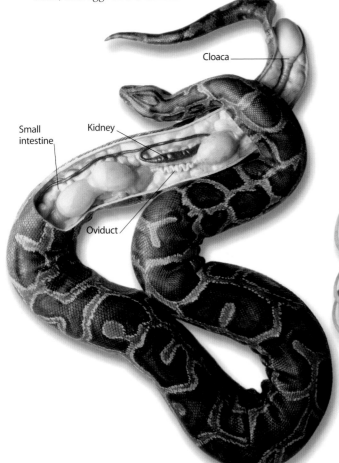

Cloaca

Small intestine

Kidney

Oviduct

▼ **THE HARD PARTS**

This python skeleton contains almost 1,000 bones. The vertebrae of all vertebrate animals protect a bundle of nerves inside called the *spinal cord*.

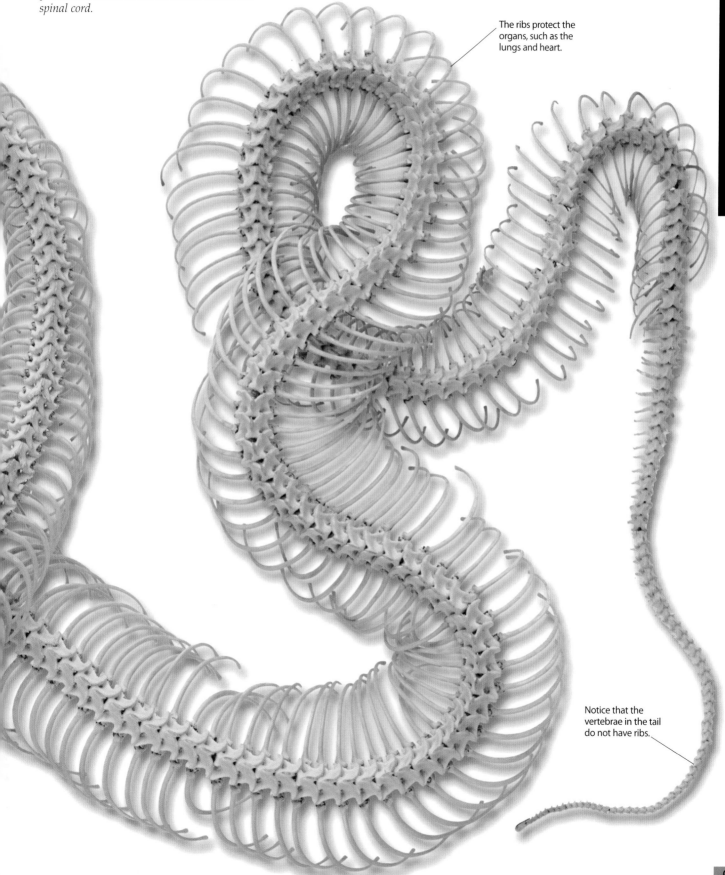

The ribs protect the organs, such as the lungs and heart.

Notice that the vertebrae in the tail do not have ribs.

DK EDUCATION

Design Miranda Brown and Ali Scrivens, The Book Makers
Managing Art Editor Richard Czapnik
Design Director Stuart Jackman
Publisher Sophie Mitchell

PEARSON

The people who made up the *DK Big Ideas of Science Reference Library* team—representing digital product development, editorial, editorial services, manufacturing, and production—are listed below.

Johanna Burke, Jessica Chase, Arthur Ciccone, Amanda Ferguson, Kathryn Fobert, Christian Henry, Sharon Inglis, Russ Lappa, Dotti Marshall, Robyn Matzke, Tim McDonald, Maria Milczarek, Célio Pedrosa, Stephanie Rogers, Logan Schmidt, Christine Whitney

CREDITS

The publisher would like to thank the following for their kind permission to reproduce their photographs:

Key: t-top; b-below/bottom; c-center; l-left; r-right; f-far; a-above

Cover and i) Dorling Kindersley: Rough Guides (roller coaster); Alamy Images: Jimmy Lopes (lettering). **ii–iii)** Corbis: Paul Hardy/Crush. **iv–v)** Corbis: O. Alamany & E. Vicens. **vi)** Dorling Kindersley: Royal British Columbia Museum, Victoria, Canada. **vii)** Corbis: Jim Reed (b); NASA: ESA/The Hubble Heritage Team/STScI/AURA (tr). **viii)** Science Photo Library: Pasieka. **x–xi)** NASA. **2** DMMP Limited/Nick Roberts Photography (b). **3** Dorling Kindersley: Judith Miller DK vintage eyeware of New York (cr); Getty Images: Time & Life Pictures (t). **4** NASA: Lunar and Planetary Laboratory (b). **4–5** Corbis: Denis Scott. **5** NASA: JPL-Caltech/R.Hurt (cr). **6–7** Getty Images: The Image Bank/Peter Adams. **7** Corbis: Peter Tumley (cr); U.S. Census Bureau (t). **8** NASA: Goddard Space Flight Center Scientific Visualization Studio. **8–9** NASA. **9** Corbis: Jim Reed/Science Faction (tl); NASA: (br). **10** Science Photo Library: Ruth Jenkinson/MIDIRS (b). **12–13** Moorfields Eye Hospital NHS Foundation Trust. **14** Getty Images. **14–15** Corbis: Liao Yujie/Xinhua Press. **15** Corbis: Roberto Tedeschi/EPA (tr). **16** Corbis: Jason Todd. **16–17** Corbis: Olivier Cadeaux. **17** Corbis: Jutta Klee. **18** Getty Images: 3D4Medical.com (cr). **20–21** NASA: CXC/M. Weiss. **21** NASA: ESA/ESO/Frederic Courbin (c). **22** Corbis: Leo Mason (b). **22–23** Corbis: Leo Mason. **23** Dorling Kindersley: Pegasus Stables, Newmarket (tl). **25** Corbis: Jeremy Horner (tr). **26** Corbis: O. Alamany & E. Vicens (bl). **26–27** Corbis: Alain LeCocq/Sygma. **28–29** Corbis: Kevin Schafer. **30–31** Corbis: Charles & Josette Lenars/Encyclopedia. **32** Corbis: Karen Kasmauski (cl). **35** Corbis: Shunichi Yamamoto/Amanaimages (br); Getty Images: Stone/Pete Turner (tl). **36** Corbis: Visuals Unlimited/Encyclopedia (tl). **36–37** Miriam Godfrey: Woods Hole Educational Institute. **37** Getty Images: David McNew/Getty Images News (br); NASA (tl). **38** Corbis: Maurizio Gambarini/DPA. **38–39** Corbis: Reg Charity. **39** Corbis: Eric and David Hosking (cr). **40** Corbis: Jonathan Blair (l); Wolfgang Kaehler (r). **41** Corbis: Scott T. Smith (l). **42** Science Photo Library: Claus Lunau Bonnier Publications (bc). **42–43** Science Photo Library: Alain Pol/ISM. **44** Corbis: Issei Kato/Reuters (bl); Lynxmotion, Inc. (br). **45** NASA (br); Robot Magazine/Maplegate Media Group: Lynxmotion, Inc. **46** Corbis: Lester Lefkowitz. **46–47** Dorling Kindersley: Rough Guides. **48** Wikipedia, The Free Encyclopedia. **49** Purdue University Libraries (t); Rube Goldberg, Inc. (br). **50** Dorling Kindersley: Natural History Museum, London (c). **51** Corbis: Dominique Aubert/Sygma/Encyclopedia (br); Dorling Kindersley: Natural History Museum, London (t). **52** Corbis: Cristobal Garcia/EPA (bl). **52–53** Corbis: Onne Van Der Wal/Terra. **53** Dorling Kindersley: Croation National Tourist Board Archive (tl). **54** Corbis: Paul A. Souders/Encyclopedia (tr). **54–55** Corbis: Roger Ressmeyer/Terra. **56** NASA: NASA Lunar and Planetary Laboratory (b). **56–57** NASA: ESA/E. Karkoschka/University of Arizona. **57** NASA (tr). **58–59** Corbis: Tim Davis/Davis Lynn Wildlife (c). **60–61** Science Photo Library: B. Murton/Southampton Oceanography Center (b). **61** Getty Images: August Sigur/Time & Life Pictures (tl); NOAA: Lophelia II 2009/ Deepwater Coral Expedition/Reefs, Rigs and Wrecks (cr). **65** Science Photo Library: Paul Zahl (tl). **66–67** Corbis: Elio Ciol/Value Art. **67** Corbis: Frank Krahmer/Latitude (cl). **69** Corbis: Kevin Schafer (cr). **70–71** Corbis: Tom Brakefield. **71** Corbis: Tim Davis/Davis Lynn Wildlife (tr). **72** Getty Images: Linda Troeller/Ovoworks/Time & Life Pictures (bl). **72–73** Dorling Kindersley: Natural History Museum, London. **74** Corbis: Carlos Ortega/EPA (cl). **74–75** Ministry of Agriculture and Food: Mari Tefre/Svalbard Global Seed Vault. **75** Corbis: Global Crop Diversity Trust/EPA (t). **77** Corbis: Denis Scott (t). **78–79** Getty Images: Panoramic Images. **79** Corbis: Stuart Westmorland/Terra (cr). **80–81** Corbis: Franck Robichon/EPA. **82** Science Photo Library: CNRI (cl); David Musher (cr). **82–83** Corbis: Aristide Economopoulos/Star Ledger (c). **84** Science Photo Library: Manfred Kage (bl). **85** Dorling Kindersley: Natural History Museum, London (tl). **86** Corbis: Liz Von Hoene/Solus (l); Getty Images: Jose Luis Pelaez/Iconica (br). **87** Corbis: Liz Von Hoene/Solus (r); Cathrine Wessel/Documentary (cl); Science Photo Library: Eye of Science (tc). **88–89** Corbis: Joe McBride/Corbis Edge. **89** Corbis: Joe McBride/Corbis Edge (b). **90–91** Corbis: Paul Hardy/Crush. **91** Corbis: Construction Photography (tl); Fritz Hoffman (cr). **92–93** Getty Images. **93** Getty Images: AFP. **96** Dorling Kindersley: Rough Guides (tr). **97** FLPA: Piotr Naskrecki/Minden Pictures (tl). **98–99** Dorling Kindersley: Natural History Museum, London.

All other images © Dorling Kindersley
For further information see: www.dkimages.com